**FREE DVD**  **FREE DVD**

Advanced Placement Human Geography
DVD from Trivium Test Prep!

Dear Customer,

Thank you for purchasing from Trivium Test Prep! We're honored to help you prepare for your AP exam.

To show our appreciation, we're offering a **FREE *AP Exam Essential Test Tips* DVD by Trivium Test Prep**. Our DVD includes 35 test preparation strategies that will make you successful on the AP Exam. All we ask is that you email us your feedback and describe your experience with our product. Amazing, awful, or just so-so: we want to hear what you have to say!

To receive your **FREE *AP Exam Essential Test Tips* DVD**, please email us at 5star@triviumtestprep.com. Include "Free 5 Star" in the subject line and the following information in your email:

1. The title of the product you purchased.

2. Your rating from 1 – 5 (with 5 being the best).

3. Your feedback about the product, including how our materials helped you meet your goals and ways in which we can improve our products.

4. Your full name and shipping address so we can send your FREE *AP Exam Essential Test Tips* DVD.

If you have any questions or concerns please feel free to contact us directly at 5star@triviumtestprep.com. Thank you!

- Trivium Test Prep Team

Table of Contents

Introduction

The AP Human Geography course is typically a year-long course, culminating in the Human Geography examination. According to the College Board's course description, the "purpose of the AP Human Geography course is to introduce students to the systematic study of patterns and processes that have shaped human understanding, use, and alteration of Earth's surface."

The goals of the AP Human Geography course are based on agreed-upon National Geography Standards, typically used at the college level. By the end of the Human Geography course or your own course of independent study in Human Geography, you should have mastered a defined set of skills. This guide provides a good general introduction to the subject - or a thorough review for students who have taken the course - but is not an adequate replacement for a class or program of independent study.

- You should be able to read and understand maps, as well as other types of geospatial data. You need to be able to employ critical thinking skills to analyze information presented in maps and geographic information systems and solve problems presented to you.
- You should develop a spatial perspective, allowing you to fully understand how different networks, cultural factors and environmental issues impact development in a given space or region.
- You must be able to use scale as a tool of critical analysis, recognizing that the same factors or events may influence things differently in a smaller or larger space, or in a local, regional, national or global context.
- You need to understand regionalization and the factors that have contributed to regionalization, including how regions are defined, how they form and how they may change over time.
- You should understand how various places relate to and interact with one another, and how different regions may be interconnected.

These essential skills will come into play in your study of Human Geography, as well as on the Human Geography examination. You may note one key, essential similarity: All of these standards require that you think critically, analyze and apply your knowledge of geography. This isn't rote memorization of place names and geographic coordinates, but a thorough understanding of the importance and implications of the study of geography.

Topics of Study

There is no single, assigned textbook for this course. Your teacher may have drawn from a number of sources to cover the topics included in the class. The Human Geography course includes the following topics, dictated by the College Board.

1. **The Nature of the Study of Geography** and **Perspectives on Geographic Study.** The following three concepts are critical to your study of geography: Space, place, and region. The course will also cover spatial organization and regionalization, and encourage students to apply geographic concepts broadly and imaginatively to recognize trends and ways in which geography has shaped the world.

2. **Migration** and **Population** is the study of human groups, how they move from place to place, and how they increase or decrease in size. Spatial and environmental factors are essential to a thorough understanding of population and migration in human geography.

3. **Cultural Interactions** and **Processes** include environmental factors on regionalization, and interaction between different regions on cultural traits and development. This is a key part of the study of human geography.

4. **Political Organization** and the political use of land has shaped not only the spaces in which we live, but also the interactions between regions within the world, both today and historically. You should expect questions concerning the political organization of space on the AP Human Geography examination.

5. **Food Production, Land Use** and **Agricultural Activity** in various regions, including the impact of environment, climate and population on the use of land for food production. This is an important part of the course and examination.

6. **Economic Development** and **Industrialization** will help you to understand the changing use of land and also how various regions have changed over time. You will need to understand, in particular, the economic differences between regions and spaces.

7. **Urban Land Use and Cities, Incorporating Settlement Patterns, The Organization and Function of Urban Spaces** and **The Importance of Urban Communities** forms a part of your understanding of geography, particularly when studied alongside the other elements and topics already discussed.

The Advanced Placement Human Geography test consists of two parts: Multiple-choice questions and free-response questions. There are 75 multiple-choice questions, making up 50 percent of your total grade. You'll have one hour in total for this portion of the test. These questions are divided into the following categories:

- **Nature and Perspectives on Geography:** 5-10%
- **Migration and Population:** 10-17%
- **Cultural Processes and Patterns:** 10-17%
- **Political Organization:** 10-17%
- **Agriculture:** 10-17%
- **Industrialization:** 10-17%
- **Urbanization:** 10-17%

The free-response portion of the examination takes up the majority of the test time, 75 minutes. There are three free-response questions in total. In the sample essays later in this text, you'll find examples of all the types of questions, along with sample answers in a high, average and low scoring range. For a high-scoring test, you need to do well on both the essay questions and the multiple-choice questions. Plan to allow 20 to 25 minutes per free-response question. Practice will help you to write well under time pressure.

You can opt to work your way through this guide and your textbook in a straightforward fashion, from beginning to end, or you may begin by taking one of the sample tests in the back of this text. If you opt to take a sample test, grade your test and assess the questions you struggled most with, devoting additional study time to those sections. When you're preparing for the test, make time to take at least one sample test in circumstances similar to those of the actual test day. Set a timer, work in a quiet room, and limit your access to supplementary materials. It is particularly important that you practice writing under pressure, given the number of questions on the exam.

Scoring

The test is scored on a scale of 1 to 5. A score of 5 is extremely well qualified to receive college credit, while a score of one is not qualified to receive college credit. While colleges and universities use scores differently, a score of 4-5 is equivalent to an A or B. A score of 3 is approximately similar to a C, while a score of 1-2 is comparable to a D or F. The examination is scored on a curve, adjusted for difficulty each year. In this way, your test score is equivalent to the same score achieved on a different year. The curve is different each year, depending upon the test. Approximately 46% of students receive a 4 or 5.

Scores of 4 to 5 are widely accepted by colleges and universities; however, scores of 3 or lower may provide less credit or none at all. More elite schools may require a score of 5 for credit and some schools' requirements vary depending upon the department. You will need to review the AP policies at your college or university to better understand scoring requirements and credit offered. While you'll take the examination in May, your scores will arrive in July. You can have your scores sent to the college of your choosing, or, if you're testing after your junior year, simply wait until you're ready to apply to the colleges of your choice.

Scoring on the multiple-choice section of the examination is straightforward. You receive one point for each correct answer. There are no penalties for an incorrect answer or a skipped question. You should, if you're unsure, guess. Even the most random guess provides you a one in four chance of a point. If you can narrow down the choices just a bit, your chances increase and, along with them, your possible test score.

The free-response questions are scored from 1-8 depending upon the quality of the essay. Essay questions are graded by human graders, typically high school and college instructors. They have been trained to grade the essays by the College Board. You'll find more information on specifics about scoring the free-response questions in the chapter that includes the sample essay questions and responses.

Staying Calm, Cool and Collected

Conquering test anxiety can help you to succeed on AP exams. Test anxiety is common and, if it's mild, can help keep you alert and on-task. Unfortunately, if you suffer from serious shakes, it may leave you struggling to focus, cause you to make careless errors, and create potential panic.

- Allow plenty of time for test preparation. Work slowly and methodically. Cramming doesn't help and will leave you depleted and exhausted.
- Remember to stay healthy. Sleep enough, eat right, and get regular exercise in the weeks preceding the AP examination, particularly if you're planning to take several tests during the same testing window.
- Practice breathing exercises to use on test day to help with anxiety. Deep breathing is one of the easiest, fastest and most effective ways to reduce physical symptoms of anxiety.

While these strategies won't eliminate test anxiety, they can help you to reach exam day at your mental best, prepared to succeed.

The night before the test, just put away the books. More preparation isn't going to make a difference. Read something light, watch a favorite show, go for a relaxing walk and go to bed. Get up early enough in the morning to have a healthy breakfast. If you normally drink coffee, don't skip it, but if you don't regularly consume caffeine, avoid it. It'll just make you jittery. Allow ample time to reach the testing location and get your desk set up and ready before the examination starts.

What to Take to the Test

- A sweatshirt or sweater, in case the testing room is cold.
- A bottle of water.
- At least two No. 2 pencils, sharpened.
- At least two black or blue ink pens.
- A wristwatch

A quick note here: there's no need to take paper along. You'll receive not only the test booklet, but also additional scratch paper to take notes and make outlines for your free-response questions. Plan to leave your phone in the car, but you may take a paperback book or magazine into the testing room if you're early.

Tackling the Test

Some people don't find testing terribly anxiety-inducing. If that's you, feel free to skip this section. These tips and techniques are designed specifically for students who do struggle with serious test anxiety:

- Control your breathing. Taking short, fast breaths increases physical anxiety. Maintain a normal to slow breathing pattern.
- Remember your test timing strategies. Timing strategies, like those discussed in relation to the free-response questions, can help provide you with confidence that you're staying on track.
- Focus on one question at a time. While you may become overwhelmed thinking about the entire test, a single question or a single passage often seems more manageable.
- Get up and take a break. Of course, this is a timed examination, so avoid this if possible! However, if you're feeling so anxious that you're concerned you

will be sick, are dizzy or are feeling unwell, take a bathroom break or get up to sharpen your pencil. Use this time to practice breathing exercises. Return to the test as soon as you're able. A little break, while it costs you some time, can sometimes clear enough mental and emotional space for you to perform well on the test.

- Remember that, while this may be an important test, it is just a test. The worst case scenario is that you do not receive college credit and find yourself taking the class in college. Even if this is the case, the knowledge you gain in this guide will put you way ahead of your peers!

The Nature of Geography and Perspectives on Geography

Human geography is the study of where human activities take place. These activities include:

- Residence
- Industrial activities
- Religious and cultural activities
- Farming

It is distinct from physical geography, which studies factors including climate and landscape; however, physical geography may affect human geography in a variety of different ways.

Human geography looks for patterns and distributions of population on the earth's surface concerning the way in which people and physical space interrelate. This is called **spatial perspective**.

Place and Region

In order to understand geography, you should thoroughly understand two key concepts: **Place** and **region**.

Place

A place is a specific point on earth, distinguished by a number of characteristics, both human and physical. Places can be identified by geographical coordinates and other means and may be large or small. For instance, Chicago, Illinois is a place, as is your AP Human Geography classroom. Places have unique locations or positions on the earth. Location can be absolute, like latitude and longitude coordinates, or relative. Relative location identifies places in relation to others. For instance, your room is down the hall from the living room or your school is two miles southwest of downtown. While anyone can understand absolute location, relative location requires that you have other knowledge about the place or surrounding places. Site and situation are also used to describe places. Site refers to internal traits, including landscape and cultural ones. Situation focuses on the context of a place, or its interconnectedness and relationships with places around it. The various traits connected to a place combine to create a personality or sense of place. For instance, Las Vegas is connected in the minds of many to gambling culture and the desert.

Regions

Regions are identified by physical and cultural traits. Regions may be small or large, but they are made up of spaces that share common physical and/or cultural traits. There are three different types of regions:

- **Formal** regions have clearly defined and identified common characteristics. These might be related to the land, like "rainforest" or to a cultural trait, like a shared language.
- **Functional** regions are connected by a movement or phenomenon. This can be cultural, like a religious movement, or natural, like a drought.
- **Perceptual** regions are linked by shared perceptions, but lack distinct, identifiable borders. Parts of the mid-South in the U.S. are commonly called the "Bible Belt"; however, there is no distinct definition of what is or is not included in the "Bible Belt".

Place and region form the basis for how we think about geography, but several key concepts are also essential for your understanding of the study of geography in this course and for the AP examination.

To guide your study of human geography, there are several important questions you can ask. While these are not all-inclusive, they will provide you with an effective overview of the subject and an idea of other questions that can inform your study and learning.

- Where are things, regions, places and cultures located?
- Why are these important?
- How do these places relate to one another, and how are they connected?
- How are humans affected by the places the live?
- How does the movement of people, information and things occur in the world?

Human Geography Tools

Geographers rely upon a wide variety of tools in the field of human geography. Many of these, but not all, are distinct from those used by other types of geographers.

- **Maps** are a basic two-dimensional representation of physical geography. Map-making is called cartography. Maps provide information about both absolute and relative location, and may also provide information about landscape features. Two-dimensional maps, by the nature of a flat representation, distort space. Three-dimensional representations, or globes, are more accurate reflections of the earth.

- **Geographic models** are used to understand and predict patterns of behavior or to record past patterns of behavior. You'll encounter a number of different geographic models during the course of a human geography class. These models may provide you with insights or information on movement, populations or other factors; however, they can have a number of weaknesses. You should, when employing a model, carefully consider cultural factors that may make that model more or less appropriate.

- **Satellite and aerial photography** provides information about human interactions with the environment, as well as natural landscapes. Today, this information is widely available, using tools like those available on Google Maps.

- **Global positioning systems (GPS)** provide specific locations or physical coordinates for places. These are absolute locations, and rely on latitude and longitude. Latitude is measured from the equator and measures horizontal position on the earth, working north or south from the equator. Longitude measures vertical position and is measured from the prime meridian, in an east or west direction. You've likely used a GPS system in your own phone or your vehicle to help you find your way from place to place. Geocaching, a popular recreational activity, also relies upon GPS.

- **Global information systems** combine information from a wide variety of sources to manage both maps and images. These computer programs make information more available and accessible than ever before, providing students and scholars with new opportunities.

Regions of the World

The map above includes the entirety of the world. For the purposes of this course, you should think less of individual nations and more of regions. In broad terms, the world can be divided into the following regions:

- The Americas
    - North America
    - Central America
    - South America
- Europe
- Asia
- The Russian Federation
- Africa
    - Sub-Saharan Africa
- Antarctica
- Oceania

Each of these regions can be further sub-divided into smaller regions.

Africa

Here, you can see the various regions of Africa, as defined by the United Nations. While these definitions are related to relative and absolute location, in many cases, there are also aspects of shared physical traits and cultural traits creating these regions and the borders between these various regions of Africa.

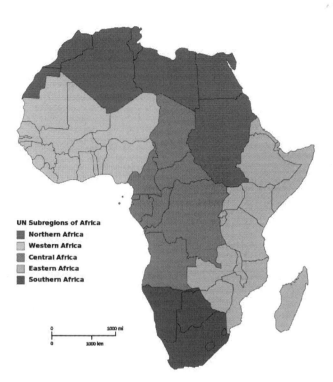

UN Subregions of Africa
- Northern Africa
- Western Africa
- Central Africa
- Eastern Africa
- Southern Africa

Latin America

Latin America, including all of South America, Central America, the Caribbean and the southernmost portion of North America is connected by shared language, shared history, and other aspects of culture.

- NORTH AMERICA
- CENTRAL AMERICA
- CARIBBEAN
- SOUTH AMERICA

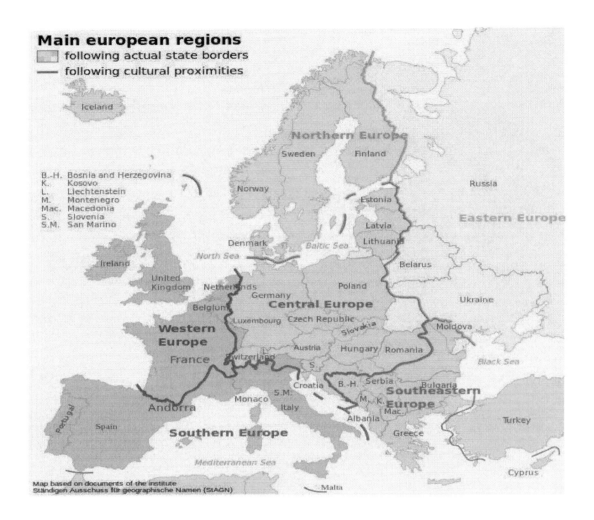

Europe

This map shows the various regions of Europe. These are perceptual regions, and may not follow national boundaries. You may notice, for instance, that the South of France is part of Southern Europe, rather than Western Europe.

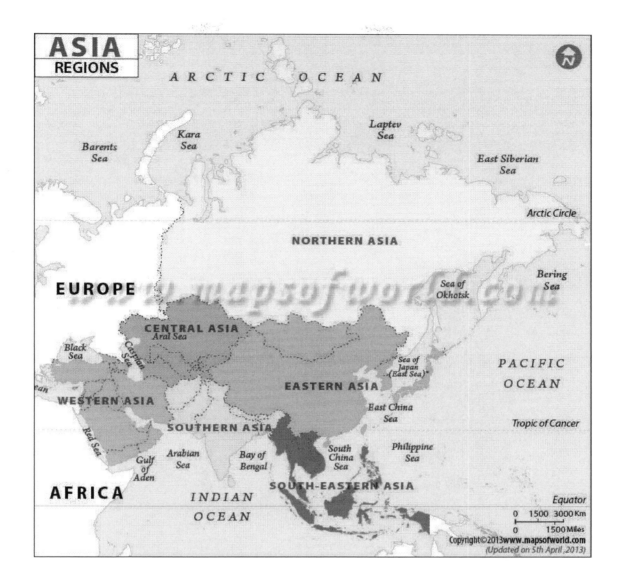

Asia

The map of Asia includes Central, Southern, Eastern and Southeastern Asia, as well as Northern and Western Asia. In this map, "Northern Asia" represents the Russian Federation and many of the former territories of the Soviet Union, which continue to share many physical and cultural traits.

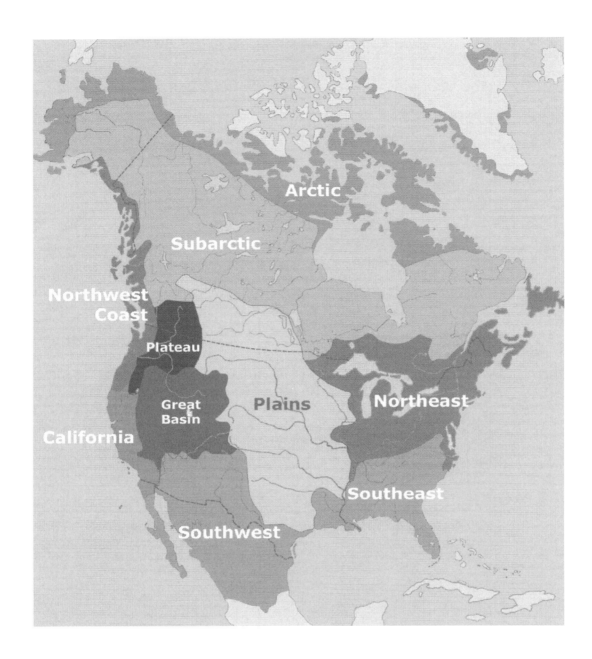

North America

North America may also be divided into a number of different regions, as seen above. While North America includes only a few countries, it is still divided into a number of regions by culture and landscape.

Absolute and Relative Location

You should work to develop a basic understanding of the absolute and relative location of various countries. This makes up a small percentage of the examination and you can succeed without this knowledge, but developing a broad understanding of which countries belong to particular regions will be helpful.

Cartography and Map-Making

Maps are more available than ever before. Today, many of us rely upon computers and smartphones to provide easily accessible maps that can guide us to our destination, whether we're driving, taking public transit or opting to walk. While modern-day map-making is high-tech, it shares many of the qualities of traditional map-making. Using maps and navigating through spaces requires spatial thinking, which is a foundational skill in studying geography. Learning how to read a map is only one step in spatial thinking, but it forms an essential foundation for your study of human geography.

There are a number of different types of maps, each serving a slightly different function. Today, you can access each of these in either print or digital formats.

Reference Maps

These are the maps that you use to navigate roads and find your way. They include city, county and state boundaries, roads, and information about the landscape. This is what most of us think of when we think of a map. Types of reference maps include:

- **Thematic Maps:** These emphasize a single quality, like climate, agricultural patterns or cultural factors.
- **Isoline Maps:** These are topographic maps, providing information about elevation and landscape.
- **Cartograms:** Cartograms are a type of map with specific, population-related distortion.
- **Choropleth Maps:** These maps provide information about a specific variable and how that variable is measured in given areas.
- **Dot Maps:** Dot maps use dots to provide information about density and numbers, from population to other factors.

Maps are also affected by their **scale, resolution, and distortion**. A globe, for instance, has little distortion and items are portrayed to-scale; however, the resolution is rather low. You cannot see smaller features on the landscape on a globe (because they usually aren't that large!) On the other hand, if you're looking at a reference map of your own community, the resolution is typically quite high.

Distortion and Projection

Distortion refers to the changes in shape that occur when a curved surface is portrayed in two-dimensions, as you would see on a paper map of the world or a specific part of the world. The type of projection used will determine the distortion in a two-dimensional map.

- **The Robinson Projection** is the most commonly used today. This projection slightly distorts all features to avoid significantly distorting any one feature and is considered a compromise projection.
- **The Gall-Peters Projection** preserves size accurately, but distorts shape significantly.
- **The Mercator Projection** depicts the shape of land masses with a high degree of accuracy, but sacrifices accurate portrayal of size and area.
- **Equidistant Projections** distort both size and shape, but accurately portray the distances between land masses.

Maps that depict larger areas, including a significant part of the world or the entire world, will experience more distortion than large-scale maps displaying a smaller area. Given this distortion, maps may be more or less accurate depending upon how the map is made, the size and scale of the map, and the projection used for the map.

You'll need to employ this understanding of mapmaking and projection in order to fully understand all elements of human geography, including studies of population, agriculture and urban development.

Migration and Population

This chapter focuses on **demographics**.

Demographics is the study of human populations and the distribution of population over time. It includes a range of subjects that can influence population, including food supply, agricultural policies, life expectancy and the movements of populations.

The human population began on a very small scale, with a number of relatively isolated human groups. Groups remained relatively small until the end of the Ice Age and progressive developments associated with the Neolithic era. With this in mind, the study of population demographics begins in earnest with the population growth associated with increased stability, settlement and improved food supplies.

In broad terms, populations are most dense in areas that support food production. These are typically mid-range latitudes. Less fertile regions, including deserts, high altitudes and tundra, support significantly smaller populations. These regions typically experience colder and hotter temperatures, less rainfall, and often have a shorter or non-existent growing season for plant foods.

Population density is measured in two different ways:

1. Population density may be measured quite directly, with the total number of people per square kilometer or square mile. This is **arithmetic density**.
2. Population density may be measured in terms of farmland or arable land, counting the total number of people per square mile or kilometer of farmland. This is **physiological density**.

Population is often portrayed in population pyramids, which show information about gender, age and proportions of populations:

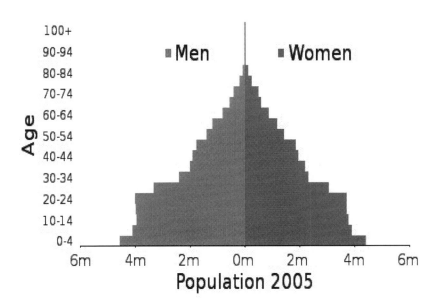

25

Examples of Population Density by Region

East Asia

Approximately one-quarter of the world's population is found in East Asia, which includes countries like China, Japan, Vietnam, Thailand and parts of Indonesia. The majority of people in these regions are farmers, working in agricultural fields; however, industry is also growing in this region of the world. While some East Asian rural areas have a low population density, the overall population density is quite high in this region, even outside of urban areas.

South Asia

South Asia is the next most populous region of the world, with countries such as India, Pakistan and Nepal. Like East Asia, populations in South Asia are largely located in the coastal regions, with substantial numbers along major rivers, and the population is predominantly agricultural.

Europe

Europe is the third most populous region and is primarily urban, rather than agricultural. Urban areas in Europe are typically consolidated near coal-mining regions.

North America

North America has a number of large cities, but much of the nation is relatively sparsely populated, unlike Europe. The highest population concentrations in North America are along the eastern coast of the United States and Canada, though there are significantly dense areas in the southwestern portion of North America, particularly in Los Angeles (in the sub-region of California) and Mexico City (in the Southwestern sub-region.)

Population Rates

Population rates have varied over time. A fertility rate of 2.1 to 2.5 children per woman is considered a **replacement rate**, creating a stable population without increase or decrease.

Birth Rates

In many parts of the world, birth rates have continually dropped since the latter part of the 20th century. Improved access to family planning services, including contraception, has affected birth rates significantly, as has a tendency to marry later and an overall increase in women's status in society. In China, a one-child policy dramatically reduced population growth, but brought a number of new social concerns. In less economically developed parts of the world, including much of Africa, birth rates continue to increase.

Mortality Rates

Death rates can also have a significant impact on population. In areas with good access to health care, life expectancies are significantly longer. Infant and child mortality also affect overall population rates in substantial ways. Average life expectancy numbers, in particular, can be altered by high infant and child mortality. Demographics is also concerned with the dependency rate. This is the total percentage of the population under 15 years of age or over 64 years of age, typically relying upon others to provide their support.

Theories of Population Change

Theories of population change are critical to your understanding of human populations. These include:

- The Demographic Transition
- Epidemiological Theories of World Health
- Malthusian Theory of Population

The Demographic Transition

The Demographic Transition is based upon Western Europe's industrial revolution and the changes that went along with it. The Demographic Transition is marked by four stages, with a clear shift in the mortality rate, moving from higher to lower. A comparable shift occurs in birth rates, with birth rates moving from higher to lower. This results, in the second stage, in an overall increase in population as the death rate decreases while the birth rate remains stable. Originally developed by Warren Thompson, this theory was improved by Frank Notestein.

This theory has a few weaknesses: Today, some European countries are experiencing a declining population, as the birth rate is less than the death rate. Additionally, the Demographic Transition assumes industrialization will occur. In some cases, particularly in less economically developed nations in Africa, there are questions as to whether industrialization is a guaranteed outcome.

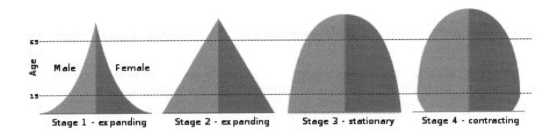

Epidemiological Theories of World Health

Epidemiology, or the study of patterns of disease, also affects population. In less economically developed countries, infectious diseases, including those spread by contaminated water, are common. In more developed counties, illnesses associated with old age and infirmity are more common, since life spans are longer.

Epidemiological population analysis can be broken into distinct stages.

1. In the transition from a hunting-gathering society to a settled society with domesticated agriculture, infectious disease appeared and became a significant factor in population demographics. Close proximity to others and animals increased the risk of disease. This stage continued until economic development allowed for the control of infectious disease.
2. Upon the advent of infection control, chronic, degenerative illnesses became a significant factor. Infectious diseases are less common; however, life spans are still not terribly long as medical care is not fully available or developed.
3. As infection control becomes reliable and widespread, generative and human-created illnesses occur. These include cancer of various types, cardiovascular disease and Type II diabetes. These illnesses are uncommon in the developing world.
4. Delayed degenerative illnesses require a significant extension of life span and occur in very old age. These illnesses require access to medical care and may be the result of medical interventions extending life.
5. In stage 5, infectious diseases re-emerge even in areas with excellent infection control, such as in developed nations. These diseases may be bacterial, viral or parasitic in nature.

Malthusian Theory of Population

Thomas Malthus is one of the best known and earliest scholars of population. In 1798, Malthus postulated that population would always exceed food supply. He believed that population grew exponentially, while food supply grew arithmetically.

Thus, Malthus believed that as food supply increased, population would increase even more.

Changes in agricultural production following World War II dramatically altered the ability to produce food, rendering Malthus' original theory incorrect. Some scholars, called Neo-Malthusians, continue to support the Malthusian theory, though evidence shows that food supply continues to increase at a higher rate than population, reducing the risk of a Malthusian Catastrophe.

Neo-Malthusians remain concerned with overpopulation, particularly in regard to the **carrying capacity** of a given region. The carrying capacity may be defined as the total ability of a given area to support a population in terms of food supply and production.

Population Control

Governments have attempted to control populations by managing the birth rate in a variety of ways. In some situations, like the early Soviet Union and Nazi Germany, individuals were encouraged to have large families. Propaganda and incentives from the government supported a higher birth rate. These are called **expansionist policies**.

Eugenics may co-exist along with expansionist policies, as in Nazi Germany. While desirable individuals were encouraged to have large families, those who did not meet strict racial guidelines were frequently involuntarily sterilized to prevent childbearing.

Restrictive policies discourage a high birth rate. These may include moderate measures, like financial incentives for smaller families and improved access to contraception, or may be more extreme, like China's one-child policy. In China, many couples have long been limited to a single child. A second child is only allowed in specific situations; families who violate the policy are punished, and forced abortion and sterilization have sometimes been used to enforce the policy. Today, China is beginning to relax these policies as a result of population issues, including significantly fewer young women than men. Some countries have fluctuated between expansionist and restrictive policies, depending upon political and religious conditions within the country.

Migration

Migration refers to human movement, particularly long-term or permanent movement from place to place. Other types of migration are associated with seasonal work or a nomadic lifestyle, for instance, following herds of animals from place to place.

Emigration is leaving a country, while **immigration** is entering a country. Migration is influenced by **push-pull factors**. Push factors encourage individuals to leave the country, while pull factors make another country more appealing. Examples of push factors include:

- Economic conditions, including recession or depression, lack of job opportunities, and low pay
- Environmental conditions, like drought or natural disasters
- Political situations, including war or the threat of war
- Cultural issues, like religious intolerance

These are all negative factors or qualities about a home country or country of origin. Individuals typically choose to leave their country of origin to seek out a better life, improved financial stability and increased personal freedom. Pull factors make another country more appealing. Examples of pull factors might include:

- Better economic opportunities, including job opportunities, higher salaries, or more ability to get and keep work
- Improved political conditions, a stable, democratic government and peaceful nation
- Cultural or religious factors, including tolerance, but also an established immigrant community
- Favorable environmental conditions, including climate and fertile land

While push/pull factors are often key reasons for immigration, immigrants often share a number of characteristics. Immigration is more likely when the distance is relatively short; young, single individuals are more likely to immigrate than families.

Immigrants are most successful in their new country when there is an established social support system, ranging from family already in the new region to a religious or cultural community. Migration is most often rural to urban, and may occur in stages. Immigrants are most likely to perceive their immigration experience accurately when the move is shorter, rather than longer.

Ravenstein's Laws of Migration

Ravenstein's Laws of Migration will be on the AP Human Geography examination. These are relatively straightforward and apply relatively well to many issues of voluntary migration. These laws, as written by Ernest George Ravenstein in "The Laws of Migration" in 1880 are:

1. Most migrants only proceed a short distance, and toward centers of absorption.
2. As migrants move toward absorption centers, they leave "gaps" that are filled up by migrants from more remote districts, creating migration flows that reach to "the most remote corner of the kingdom."
3. The process of dispersion is inverse to that of absorption.
4. Each main current of migration produces a compensating counter-current.
5. Migrants proceeding long distances generally go by preference to one of the great centers of commerce or industry.
6. The natives of towns are less migratory than those of the rural parts of the country.
7. Females are more migratory than males.

Migrations' Impact on Population

Immigration can have a substantial impact on population. For instance, in the 19th century, the United States grew in population largely because of the immense influx of immigrants. These immigrants hoped for improved financial opportunities, religious tolerance, and to avoid oppressive governments. Prior to 1840, some 90 percent of immigrants to the United States were British. Between 1840 and 1910, many western and northern Europeans moved to the United States, while the period from 1910 to 1930 saw a large number of southern and eastern European immigrants. Since 1950, Latin American and Asian immigrants make up the majority of immigrants to the United States. Many moved to ethnic communities, where they could continue to speak their own language, eat local foods and practice traditional cultural customs.

It is also critical to note that immigration is not always voluntary. Many individuals were brought into the United States and Latin America from Africa involuntarily, in the chains of slavery. This is called **forced migration**. Forced migration also moved groups of Native Americans from their homes to reservations in different locations. The Trail of Tears is an example of one such forced migration. Forced migration is not impacted by push/pull factors.

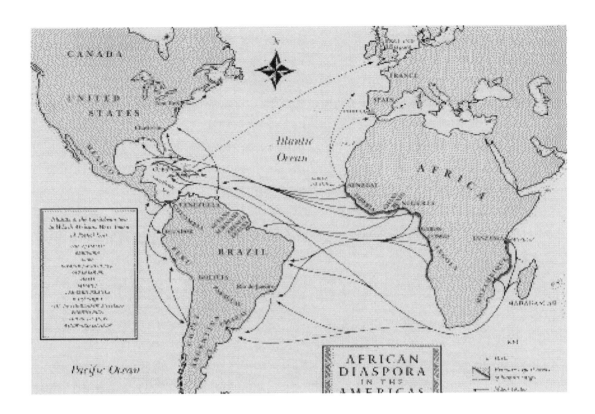

Internal Migration

Migration may also occur within a single nation. The westward expansion of the United States is an example of **internal migration** as is the flight of large numbers of African-Americans to the northern U.S. to avoid Jim Crow laws and rampant racism in the South. Internal migrations may be individual and spread out over time or can occur in relatively large numbers in a short time, like the wagon trains that moved families west in the 19th century. Individuals typically move within a single country for the same reasons as people immigrate to another nation, seeking a better life, improved job opportunities or increased personal freedom.

Immigration Policy

Countries control immigration with laws and regulations. These typically limit the number of immigrants allowed into the country, and often on the number of immigrants from certain countries, as well. Many countries have regulations and rules regarding the educational and income background of immigrants. It is, for instance, easier for someone with a college degree to emigrate to another country than for someone without education.

This has, at times, led to a "**brain drain**", as large numbers of educated people leave countries looking for a better life. Some countries may offer preferential treatment to individuals who have particular and appealing job skills, and most countries offer preference to family members of residents or citizens. While immigration regulations vary from country to country, one of the most unusual is the Israeli immigration policy. All Jews have the right of return to Israel and may enter the country and take up residence at any time. Political changes in Europe now allow any citizen of the European Union to live and work in any EU country regardless of citizenship and legal residence.

Legal residence is the first step in immigration; however, many immigrants hope, eventually, to become citizens. Legal immigration is, in many nations, a challenging prospect, taking a great deal of time and money.

Guest worker status is an option in some countries. Guest workers commonly come from less economically developed nations and do jobs that are deemed unappealing to many citizens in the country accepting the immigrant. Work permits allow an individual to live and work in the country for a set period of time, or while employed by a particular employer.

Involuntary Emigration

There are many reasons that people leave their home countries for a new one. They include better economic opportunities, or to escape violence and persecution.

For many, the risks associated with **illegal immigration** are worthwhile. Those who have emigrated illegally are referred to in the United States alternately as "illegal immigrants" and "undocumented workers," often depending on ideological affiliation. While these people have broken the laws of their new country by entering through extralegal means, their lives are almost always better than they would otherwise be in the country they came from, which provides a powerful incentive.

While voluntary and extralegal/illegal emigration is typically something that people plan for, **refugees** usually leave their countries involuntarily, the violence of war, or because they fear persecution on the basis of race, religion, nationality, social group or political opinions.

Refugees are often forced to flee leave their homes with no preparation and few possessions. They typically have no legal standing, leaving their countries without even basic legal paperwork. Many flee their homes on foot in an attempt to avoid danger, but they may also travel by bicycle, car, boat or even public transit. During times of civil war, refugee camps are often established outside of the war zone or across a national border.

Refugee camps are commonly run by international organizations, other nations, or charitable groups and provide shelter, health care and food to those fleeing a war zone. In some countries, an individual with refugee status may have preferential status with regard to immigration. In many cases, refugees are unable to return to their home or may have no home to return to, requiring assistance in eventual resettlement in another country. Today, there are significant ongoing refugee crises in a number of areas, including parts of Africa, the Middle East and Eastern Europe. According to the United Nations, in 2004, there were as many as 24 million refugees.

Summary

Population is impacted by birth rates, death rates and life expectancy, as well as migration. The population of a country may drop due to famine, higher death rates, or mass emigration, while population may increase as infant mortality drops, life expectancies increase and disease is better managed. Increased immigration also results in a higher population. Individuals migrate in search of improved living conditions, with the exception of forced migrations and refugees. Forced migrants move under threat of immediate violence, while refugees flee for their lives, avoiding civil war or persecution. Understanding all of these factors will help you to recognize the importance of the study of human geography.

Cultural Interactions and Processes

Culture is a multidimensional human creation, one that both creates a clear sense of place and arises and exists because of specific places. There are many different aspects of culture. These include:

- Language
- Religion
- Traditional, folk and popular culture

Together, these elements combine to create the identities we connect to places. Culture provides places with personality and character. These factors affect how people speak, perceive the world around them, interact with one another and their environment, and often what they eat. Music, literature, and art are all part of traditional and popular culture. When you think of a place – even home – your mental image involves cultural factors. For instance, the city of Vienna, Austria is connected to the German language, sausage and pastry, classical music, and baroque architecture, but also to the history of World War I and II, and modern pop culture. These elements make up the city in the same way as its urban design, architecture and landscape.

When you think of your home, you may think of particular buildings such as churches, signs in the English language (or in others, if you live in a multilingual area,) or events like the county fair, which features many traditional American cultural elements, such as rodeos, country music and traditional American food.

Culture can occur on a large-scale, like a national, regional or even smaller scale. Immigrant neighborhoods, like Chinatowns found in many major U.S. cities, provide the language, religious traditions, foods and goods connected with another region within the scope of a single neighborhood. Regional cultures may be connected by shared language or religion. In a country, there may be multiple cultures coexisting within national boundaries or exceeding those boundaries.

Ethnicity

Often, culture is linked to ethnicity. Ethnicity relates to a particular ethnic group, which is defined by shared traits, including customs and traditions, religion, language and race. Ethnicities can span across many of these traits – for instance, Jews share a common religion, customs and traditions, but may differ racially, geographically and culturally. Ethnicity may sometimes also be linked to political organization.

Ethnicities are linked to a particular place, either legally or through custom and practice. Culture may be linked to ethnicity, but is, like political boundaries, not always linked to it.

Culture includes both material and non-material culture. Material culture includes physical goods, like houses, clothing and consumer goods. Material culture includes both folk and traditional aspects of culture, and popular culture.

Folk or traditional culture is most likely to be:

- Shared through oral tradition
- Unchanging or slowly changing
- Distinct from other cultural traditions
- Rural, rather than urban
- Homes and structures mesh with the landscape and rely upon natural materials

While folk culture is distinctive, rural and slow to change, pop culture is the opposite. Typically found in urban areas, popular culture changes rapidly and is widespread over large geographic areas. Popular culture is shared in a variety of ways, including mass media and the internet. Examples of popular culture might include:

- Wearing jeans
- Pop music
- Social media

Non-material goods include language, religion, culture and tradition. Material culture may, in some cases, reflect the importance of some aspects of non-material culture. Innovation or technological change can drive differences in material culture, but may impact non-material culture over time.

Cultural Diffusion

Components of culture are transmitted through **diffusion** in one of several ways:

- Contagious diffusion
- Hierarchical diffusion
- Stimulus diffusion
- Relocation diffusion

The diffusion of popular culture, no matter the method of diffusion is fundamentally destructive to traditional or folk culture. The modern proliferation of pop culture through mass media and the Internet, combined with the phenomenon of globalization, has already caused many traditional and folk cultures to become obsolescent, and many more are threatened now.

Language

Language, broadly defined, is a form of spoken communication, understood by both the speaker and the listener. Language changes over time, and may (depending upon conditions) eventually become a new language, incomprehensible by speakers of the original language.

Within a society, language changes as a result of two distinct factors: migration and isolation. Migration can impact both the language of the region individuals are emigrating to, as well as the language of the migrants.

Migrants may adapt some of the linguistic traits of their new nation. In regions with large immigrant populations, words from immigrant languages may enter the original language. In some cases and depending upon the region, languages may remain similar with regional differences, called **dialects**. Dialects are part of a single language.

Sometimes, dialects develop into entirely new languages. Isolation will also, over time, impact language. For instance, if a group has relatively little contact with outsiders or other native speakers, the language may change over generations, leading to a new dialect or even a new, independent language.

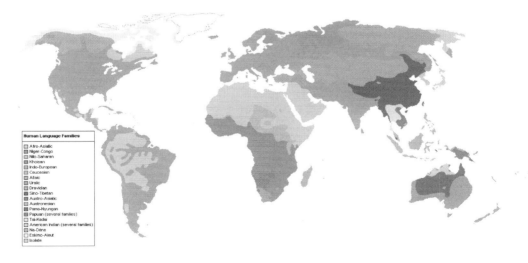

How Language Changes

Languages are divided into families, branches and groups. Language families have a common ancestor language. You may, for instance, find it relatively easy to understand Italian if you can speak Spanish, because they are both based on Latin, the now-dead language of the Roman Empire, but they are distinct languages with their own rules, grammar and vocabulary.

Within a group, there are individual languages, and within each language, there are dialects and accents. Similar languages may share some vocabulary or grammar; while some words or usages may differ, if you can speak a language, you can understand a regional dialect (perhaps with some difficulty.) Once you move outside of a language group, languages will differ progressively more and become far more different.

Languages changes over time; however, history can be traced through our use of language and the way languages have spread and changed. The factors that have clearly affected language and the development of different languages include:

- War and conquest - for example, when the French-speaking Norman William the Conqueror conquered England, a large number of French words entered the language
- Integration and isolation of various cultures can lead to similar or very different languages
- Physical and political boundaries may impact both isolation and integration.

Geographical features play a significant role in defining the distribution of languages. Areas near one another often share the same language family or language group, particularly if they have been affiliated politically. You may, for instance, notice that the Indo-European language family includes not just European countries, but modern-day Iran and India. The groups within the Indo-European language family include the Romance languages, the Germanic languages, the Balto-Slavic languages and the Indo-Iranian languages. You may be able, in this, to consider the history of this region of the world and recognize a shared history over time, including periods of conquest and land-based trade routes.

Language is an essential part of culture; it responsible for not only the basic transmission of information, but also a wide range of other cultural components. Language transmits culture from generation to generation, and even alters thoughts and perceptions. The words we use can change how we engage with our environment and what we think about the world around us.

Today, as the world becomes a smaller and more global place, many languages have disappeared and others are disappearing, such as Yiddish, a language traditionally spoken by Ashkenazi (German and Northern European) Jews, and Gaelic, a language traditionally spoken in Ireland.

Religion

Religion is popularly understood as the belief in a god or a group of gods, or in a supernatural force of some kind. It usually involves an organized system of beliefs, ceremonies, and rules used to worship a supernatural power, or an interest, belief, or activity that is very important to a person or group. Religious anthropologists still debate the exact definition of a religion to this day.

For the purposes of human geography, we will discuss not only religion, but also **religious landscape**, which includes religious rites, rituals, practices and geographic holy sites. There are a number of religions and religious landscapes in regions across the world that play an essential role in culture and dramatically affect politics and personal identity.

Classifications of Religion

Religions are often categorized as **monotheistic** or **polytheistic**. A monotheistic religion believes in a single deity. The world's Abrahamic religions (Christianity, Islam and Judaism) are all monotheistic. A polytheistic religion believes in multiple deities. The religion of ancient Greece was polytheistic, as is modern Hinduism.

Religions usually have a **cosmogony** or origin story. The most familiar cosmogony to Americans that describes the origin of the Earth is the story in Genesis, in which God creates the heavens and the earth within a period of seven days.

Religions may be **universalizing** or **ethnic**. Typically, ethnic religions are more closely connected to land and geography. They may be relevant only in a particular region and lack a specific founder or origin. Examples of ethnic religions include Judaism and Hinduism.

A universalizing religion has an identified founder, holidays based on the founder's life, and are often widely distributed throughout the globe. Examples of universalizing religions include Christianity, Islam and Buddhism[1].

---

[1] There are some that do not consider Buddhism a religion, but rather a philosophy. Since the majority of Buddhists practice Buddhism as a religion, it is considered as such on the AP Examination.

Within a single universalizing religion, there are often **branches**, **denominations** and **sects**. For instance, Catholicism, Eastern Orthodoxy and Protestantism are all branches of Christianity. Within those branches, Episcopalians and Baptists are denominations of Protestantism.

Sects are smaller divisions within faiths and are typically closely related to a denomination, but tend to be somewhat more radical and/or to have a fundamental disagreement with their most closely related denomination.

On the AP examination, you should have a basic familiarity with the major world religions, including:

- **Christianity** was founded by the apostles of Jesus Christ in the first century of the Common Era. Christianity spread slowly until its acceptance by the Roman Emperor Constantine in the early 4th century C.E., and spread rapidly through most of the world thereafter. Today, it is the largest religion in the world, with roughly one-third of the world's population identifying as Christian.
- **Islam** is the second largest religion in the world, with roughly one-fifth of the world's population identifying as Muslim. Founded in the 7th century C.E. in the land today identified as Saudi Arabia, during the lifetime of the Prophet Muhammad, Muhammad's visions and writings form the basis for Islam, which, like Christianity, spread rapidly after its founding.
- **Hinduism**: An ethnic, polytheistic religion founded in India between 2300 and 1500 BC, it is the world's third largest religion, with almost a billion people identifying as Hindus. Hinduism is still mostly practiced in India. Many Hindus also consider themselves Buddhist, as neither religion prevents its adherents from identifying with several faith traditions.
- **Buddhism**: A universalist religion that originated near Nepal and spread outward to India, China, Japan and beyond, it is the world's fourth largest religion. There are two significant branches in Buddhism: Theravada and Mahayana. Theravada Buddhism is significantly more proscriptive than Mahayana. Buddhism is the fourth largest religion in the world, though many Buddhists also consider themselves Hindus, as neither religion prevents its adherents from identifying with several faith traditions.
- **Judaism**: An ethnic religion that began in the land today identified as Israel, it is a monotheistic faith identified as one of the three religions of the Book, alongside Christianity and Islam (these three are also called Abrahamic religions.) It is the world's sixth largest religion (after Sikhism, which is not covered on the AP Examination) and though the year of its founding is contested – it is one of the world's oldest monotheistic religions – it was

42

codified into a definitively organized religion sometime around 1500 BC. Judaism spread across the world during the Diaspora in 70 C.E., when Roman Empire forcibly split the Jewish population and forced them to migrate to different areas throughout the Roman Empire.

Religion and Culture

Religion can shape culture in a number of ways. In many cases, religion shapes the morality of a nation, including the rules of behavior and relationships in society. As religions spread, other aspects of culture, including language, may spread from region to region. For instance, the religious text of Islam, the Qur'an[2], is written in Arabic. Prior to the spread of Islam, there were a number of different languages throughout the region. The need to read the Qur'an and to speak with others of the same faith made Arabic significantly more common as a language, spreading it throughout the Middle East and beyond to many parts of Africa and Central Asia.

The Religions of the World

Anthropologists have discovered that a belief in the supernatural – a prerequisite for religion – began quite early in history and has been present in every human culture that we have yet studied.

While we know little about prehistoric belief, modern hunter-gatherer societies typically practice animism, sometimes called shamanism. The core belief in animism

---

[2] Also spelled Koran and Quran, depending on translation.

is that all things, from people and animals to plants and stones, have a spirit. Rituals and religious practices are used to appease these spirits. Today, around ten percent of Africans continue to practice traditional animism, and other animists are scattered in populations around the world.

While animism forms the basis of many early polytheistic religions, polytheism remains a part of major religions today, particularly for Hindus. Animistic and polytheistic religions are typically ethnic, but, ethnic religions do not have to be polytheistic. Judaism shares many of the traits of ethnic religions, but is strictly monotheistic. Most ethnic religions do not **proselytize**, or attempt to spread their religion, gain followers or share their religion's message with non-believers.

Universalist religions usually seek to spread and gain followers through missionary activities. Buddhism, Christianity Islam and spread quickly from their original regions and continue to spread today.

Religious differences have led to significant conflict, both historically and today. In particular, conflicts between Christianity and Islam have been a shaping factor historically, altering the way nations and cultures relate to one another from the early days of Islam, through the Crusades, the Ottoman Empire and today.

Modern Religious Trends

Two religious trends coexist in the modern world. The first of these is **secularization**. Secularization ranges from atheism to agnosticism to a simple lack of interest in religion or spirituality, and is common in much of Europe, urban areas in the United States, China and the former Soviet Union.

On the other hand, **fundamentalism** is also prevalent in many areas of the world. Fundamentalism is independent of any particular religion, though it is most common in Christianity and Islam. Fundamentalism is usually expressed as a reactionary (anti-modern) religious outlook with a strong propensity for involvement in politics, advocating for laws, policies and governments based on religious precepts. While many religious denominations have relatively little interest in politics, fundamentalist religious groups often believe that their faith and practice of faith is the only correct way to live and practice, and extend this belief into all aspects of their daily life.

Political Organization

Human geography includes the study of the political use of space, or how we divide spaces into nations with **boundaries**. While, in some cases, national boundaries relate to the landscape, in many others, they do not. Political boundaries may alter how places relate to one another and interact, how different ethnicities relate within a single nation and how people interact with their environment.

Today, there are more than 200 unique political entities, or countries, in the world. These range from very large countries, like China and the United States, to very small countries. Colonial empires of the 19th century eventually fell over the course of the 20th century, leaving young nations struggling with new independence. As various larger powers, including the Soviet Union, have collapsed, many new, smaller nations have been created. Some nations have large amounts of coastline, available for trade, while others have very little or none at all. Nations may be closely allied with their neighboring states, or have a difficult and contentious relationships. Disputes over boundaries are quite common.

Race and Organization

Racial and ethnic tensions may add to political conflict both within and outside of individual states. Biologically, race is of very little importance. From a genetic standpoint, the differences that define one race of people from another are negligible at best. Historically, race is of significantly greater importance, involved in a number of atrocities, particularly slavery. Racism remains a factor in many regions, from the United States to Africa.

Race as a concept has been thoroughly debunked from a biological standpoint, but its social implications are vast. Historically, race was defined on the basis of physical features, including skin tone, facial features, and hair type. Traditionally, humans were divided into four races, one originating in Asia, one in Africa, one in Europe, and one in Southeast Asia.

Anthropologists and human geologists are now uncomfortable with the subject of race, and are divided: Some still see value in race as a social and political construct, while others find it relatively useless and not a relevant factor in study. These individuals would opt to use ethnicity as a primary trait, rather than race. Race is becoming less classifiable, as people increasingly form multi-racial families.

We cannot understand political organization without developing some understanding of the lasting impact of race. Racial discrimination has impacted countries around the world; however, the strongest impact has been on the African continent. Slavery, of course, depleted the population of Africa, causing significant human and cultural loss. White colonists from Britain and elsewhere established colonies throughout Africa, particularly in the 19th century, leading to a loss of traditional leadership and significant and lasting political challenges.

Race, Segregation and Colonialism

Colonialism also significantly impacted, depleted or destroyed the aboriginal populations of the Americas, Australia and New Zealand, as well as parts of Asia and Southeast Asia. Colonialism relied upon a basic and fundamental racism. In order to colonize a nation, the colonial power had to hold, as a key belief, an idea of racial superiority. This ranged from viewing the native populations of the Americas as sub-human, to taking on an imperial status and believing that bringing European people and culture to a region would improve things, because the people needed that assistance, given their "weaknesses."

Racial segregation is not limited to the past. Racial segregation continued, via the Jim Crow laws, through a significant part of the 20th century in the United States and still remains a de facto reality in many parts of the U.S., particularly major urban areas like Detroit and large areas in the South. While segregation is no longer dictated by law, economics and other factors play a role in the United States and elsewhere. Throughout much of the 20th century, extreme racial segregation existed in South Africa under a policy called apartheid.

Ethnicity and Organization

Ethnicity is less recognizable by physical traits. While ethnic groups may share broad physical traits, like similar skin coloring, these are frequently seen in other groups as well. Ethnic groups self-identify in many cases, on the basis of shared language, religion and culture. In immigrant groups, they may live near one another, forming communities to preserve their culture. Ethnicity is typically identified on the basis of long-lasting cultural traditions, but some individuals may feel more connected to their ethnicity than others. Recognizing and understanding the differences and similarities between racial and ethnic groups will help you to understand the political aspects of human geography.

States, Nations and Nation-States

There are several different political entities in the world today and you need to be familiar with each. Below, you will find each of these types of entities, along with a description and explanation.

States are **independent political entities**. Typically, in geographical terms, a state is a synonym for a nation; however, there are some exceptions to this, including some territories that are not considered nations. An independent state is not the same as one of the United States, which defers to a single, central government. In the US, "states" have individual state governments, but are not independent political entities.

An independent state is an organized political entity with a single, centralized government. In this sense, the US is a single state. Independent states, by definition, have a number of rights and responsibilities.

- States tax citizens
- States provide services to citizens, like maintaining roads, providing a justice system, and making laws
- States raise armies and may require military service
- States can only exist if the people believe in the existence of the state and share a national identity
- State governments may vary, but are typically federal or unitary. In a federal system, individual territories have significant rights. In a unitary system, those rights are only granted by the state governing body

States are the broadest heading for a defined area within human geography. Students should also be aware of the following terms:

- Nation - Has a shared language and culture, similar ethnic background and a common political system.
- Nation-state – Commonly used to mean a country, this should have a single government, a shared commitment to a status as a nation-state, and a shared history. Ethnic backgrounds and languages may differ within a nation-state; however, the state is united by shared emotional ties among its citizens.
- Multinational states - Multiple nations with different identities, governments and cultures live within a single state. This is quite likely to lead to conflict, as seen in the Balkan Wars of the 1990s. Conflict within multinational states can be particularly brutal.
- Stateless nations - In a stateless nation, the people have a shared commitment to the nation, but the nation lacks land or sovereignty. Palestine is the best-known example of a stateless nation, but there are many others, including the Kurds in Iraq, the Tibetans in China and various aboriginal groups in Australia.

The Geography of the State

The geographic characteristics of states can vary widely. States can be different sizes, shapes, have access to different resources and be governed differently. In terms of size, both geographically and demographically, states range from very large to very small. The shape of states may be categorized in several different ways.

- In a **compact** state, all parts of the state are approximately the same distance from the physical center of the state. Poland is an example of a compact state.
- A **fragmented** state is made up of two or more land masses, separated by water. The Philippines are fragmented, consisting of multiple islands.
- An **elongated** state is a single piece of land, but it has a long and narrow shape, like Vietnam.
- **Prorupted** states are mostly compact, with a single extending branch of land.
- A **perforated** state has a piece of another state within its borders. Italy, home to the Vatican state, is an example of a perforated state.
- An **exclave** is a part of a state located within another state
- An **enclave** is an independent state located within another state.

Most states around the globe have access to some amount of coastline, enabling trade and travel by sea. A relatively small number of states lack any coastal land. These states are landlocked and include parts of Europe, Asia, Africa and South America. In Europe, wide, navigable rivers allow for trade, even in landlocked countries, but this is not necessarily true in all regions.

Boundaries between countries develop in various ways, including through natural geography, like rivers or mountains, simple geometric straight lines or cultural divisions. Boundaries are typically defined in writing first, then delimitated on maps, and finally, **demarcated** with fences or man-made markers showing where one state ends and another one begins. Boundaries between states typically extend to waterways, subterranean resources, and airspace. The boundaries between states can precede the states, like those boundaries that are geographic. Boundaries can be superimposed, dividing single cultures into different states. Subsequent boundaries have been renegotiated or altered over time, through war and other human events. A **relic boundary** is no longer politically relevant, but is still visible in some way, through extant markers, walls or fences.

Irredentism is the expansion of state boundaries. This often occurs as the result of superimposed boundaries. The cultures divided by these boundaries seek to reunite themselves in a single nation. In many cases, both states will attempt to claim the territory, leading to violence or territorial disputes.

Cultural Factors

States may be closely unified by a variety of cultural factors, but can also be drawn apart and weakened by differences. Those factors that support unity are called **centripetal forces**, while **centrifugal forces** pull societies apart.

- Centrifugal forces include cultural, linguistic and religious difference, economic disparity and geographic differences, including access to resources. Centrifugal forces are sometimes called **devolutionary**.
- Centripetal forces include a strong central government, education, ideology, and alliances against an external force or enemy.

In some cases, centrifugal forces may become so strong as to tear apart a nation-state, leading to political conflict, the collapse of nations or nation-states, and even civil war. In recent years, the Soviet Union and the communist empire of Eastern Europe collapsed as a result of varied centrifugal forces. These forces included increased multiculturalism, closer ties with the West and growing economic disparity.

In some extreme cases, the cultural, religious, ethnic or linguistic differences within a state may lead to extreme violence. Genocide is mass murder on the basis of religion, ethnicity, or political ideology. While the Holocaust is the best-known genocide and was responsible for international recognition of genocide, genocides have also occurred elsewhere and some regions today are at risk of genocide.

Geopolitics

Geopolitics is the study of the impact of geography on politics, particularly international politics and international relations. Geopolitics integrates the study of different subjects, including the social sciences, political sciences and geography. For the purposes of the AP Human Geography exam, you should be aware of several major scholars and movements in the field of geopolitics. The term was first developed early in the 20th century, but the field had already taken shape by that time.

Historical Geopolitical Theory

Ratzel's Theory

The German scholar **Friedrich Ratzel** was particularly interested in the shared interactions of anthropology, geology and political science. Ratzel believed that nation-states were organic and would, as organic bodies, grow as needed, annexing other territories. He believed borders were changeable and prone to continue to change. Ratzel developed the notions of "**raum**" or space and "**lebensraum**" or living space. Deeply influenced by social Darwinism, according to the doctrine of "lebensraum" the dominant group would gain space by taking over lands of less-dominant or lesser peoples. This concept influenced the Nazi desire to create a large German empire.

Mahan's Theory

The British and American schools of geopolitics are significantly different than the German school. In reading about these schools, consider their later political implications in light of both World Wars, as well as the Cold War.

Alfred Mahan was a U.S. naval officer and historian, writing in the late 19th and early 20th century. Mahan theorized that the power that controlled the sea would dominate foreign powers. This theory suggested that **sea power** or naval power was the most essential part of political dominance, both commercially and during times of war. Given this, control of sea ports was especially critical. His theories remain important for the U.S. Navy today, but played a particularly large role in the desire for naval dominance before and during World War I.

The Heartland Theory

Around the beginning of the 20th century, **Sir Halford Mackinder** developed the **Heartland Theory**. According to Mackinder's theory, the most important region in the world was what he defined as the Heartland. The Heartland included Central and Western Europe, Eastern Europe and into the Western part of Russia and the Ukraine. Mackinder envisioned a land-based empire, composed of the "World-Island." The World-Island included Eurasia and Africa. All other lands were considered peripheral. A great power centered in the Heartland would be able to defeat these lands on the periphery; Mackinder's theory was embraced by Germany and the Soviet Union, but it is no longer relevant. The Heartland Theory required a sole reliance on sea power; after the advent of air-based weaponry, the theory became outdated.

The Rimlands Theory

Nicholas Spykman actively disagreed with Mackinder. In the 1940s, Spykman theorized that the "rimlands" of Eurasia were the most critical for international dominance. The "rimlands" include year-round accessible harbors and ports. His work is a product of the Cold War era and was distinctly concerned with controlling the potential westward spread of the Soviet Union.

Modern Geopolitical Theory

Modern geopolitical theory is referred to commonly as meta-geopolitics. This theory is broken down into several distinct aspects.

1. Domestic politics
2. Social and health issues
3. Environment
4. Economics
5. International relations
6. Military and security issues
7. Human potential and science

These tools can be applied to states, provinces, regions and even entities without political power. These are the tools a state uses to maintain its power, fundamentally.

Geopolitics is commonly interested, as you can see in the above theories, in the world order, or who holds power and how power is held within the world and international community.

- A bipolar world order dominated after World War II. The two powers were, in this case, the United States and U.S.S.R.
- A multi-polar world order has many different powers, each acting independently or working in alliances with one another.
- States may act unilaterally, or without international support.

Containment

During the Cold War, Western powers, and the United States in particular, relied upon a policy of containment. Containment was designed to prevent the spread of communism. Containment theory is less a geopolitical theory and more an applied series of policies.

The Domino Theory

The Domino Theory is also an applied theory, rather than a specifically geopolitical one. According to the Domino Theory, destabilization is likely to spread from state to state. In the late 20th century, the progressive destabilization of Eastern Europe and the Soviet Union is an example of the Domino Theory in practice. In some cases, the fear of the **domino effect** has led to military action by international powers.

Economics

While world power and organization is one factor in the study of geopolitics, economics also form a key part of the study of geopolitics and play an essential role in the international relations between states in the world today. Again, a key theory guides our understanding of global economics today. Immanuel **Wallerstein's World Systems Theory** is the most critical for your understanding of the global economy.

World Systems Theory

Wallerstein treats the global economy as a single entity, with a single market and a global division of labor. According to Wallerstein, goods and resources move from the periphery to the core. His is a three-tier system, with a core, semi-periphery and periphery. Wallerstein's theory was heavily impacted by European colonialism, but is not an inaccurate representation of the modern economy. For Wallerstein, the periphery is made up of less-developed states and the core of more-developed states. Today, the United States is the most important core country, but not the only core country.

Several key terms may appear in discussions of economics in human geography. You may already be familiar with these, but should know them if you do not currently.

- **Capitalism** is a free market economic system, with the goal of making a profit on goods or services sold.
- **Commodification** is the process of putting a cost or price on a good or service.
- **Colonialism** is a historical term, by which western governments established colonies and took control of less-developed nations. Colonialism created the global economy and defined the periphery of that economy.

The **progressive globalization** of the world is a key factor in our modern understanding of human geography and political organization. Today, **supranational organizations** play a key role in the political organization and international relations between states. States participate in supranational organizations voluntarily, typically agreeing to forfeit some amount of independence in exchange for their participation. Some supranational organizations, like the United Nations, have the power to act in various situations, for instance, to prevent genocide, implement international sanctions, regulate laws concerning international waters and send in teams to investigate or work to keep the peace throughout the world. Many other supranational organizations concern economic or political issues within a larger economy or smaller region of the world. Examples of supranational organizations include the European Union, NATO, the Common Market and OPEC.

In order to understand human geography, you must recognize how our world is organized into various political entities. These states have defined borders, governments, and varied relationships with other states. Geopolitics attempts to explain the world order, or dominance among the states in various ways. Many of these theories are no longer relevant, as the world has changed with the invention of air travel and weaponry. Economic theories are also a part of the study of geopolitics, explaining economic dominance as one part of international relations.

Food Production and Agriculture

Agriculture and **food production** is an essential part of human life and has been since the beginning of civilization. Like many other aspects of human culture and life, the geography of the place in which the people live impacts how they produce food, what foods they produce and what they eat.

Agriculture is the intentional tending of crops and livestock for food production. While we may not often think of it, agriculture is a relatively modern innovation. In order to produce food using agricultural methods, humans often alter the natural landscape, clearing forests to plant crops, introducing new irrigation methods, and today, using chemicals to control the plants and insects that live in the region. Agriculture shapes how land is used, how villages and later towns develop, and how we live.

The Development of Agriculture

For many millennia, human populations subsisted by hunting animals, fishing and gathering naturally-growing plant foods, including grains, vegetables, tubers, fruits and nuts. Food production was the dominant activity of the entire human community. In many cases, groups lived nomadically, following herds of animals as they moved seasonally or in search of new food supplies. Newer research shows that these groups also routinely exploited available plant foods, and in some regions, relatively large amounts.

Food supplies were variable and there were limited means of storing food. Available food depended upon the environment, and groups used those foods available in their region, from fish to meat to plants. In wetter and warmer climates, food was more accessible.

Food production used a variety of specialized **tools**, typically made of stone or bone for Paleolithic groups and from various metals for later hunting and gathering populations. Early tools included throwing spears, harpoons, knives and blades for butchering, axes of various sorts and fishing-related items, including baskets and nets. Today, a very few small populations continue to live through hunting and gathering, including the Bushmen of the Kalahari Desert in Africa. All communities of hunters and gatherers were, by necessity, quite small. This lifestyle did not provide for larger, settled communities.

The transition from a hunting-and-gathering lifestyle to a settled and agricultural one occurred during the Neolithic period. At first, it is likely that humans tended naturally growing plants, before intentionally saving seeds and planting crops.

The beginning of agriculture marks the beginning of the Neolithic period and a time of great innovation. The first plants were likely domesticated in Southeast Asia and were primarily tubers, starting around 14,000 years ago. Agriculture spread relatively rapidly into Southwest Asia around 10,000 years ago, with the domestication of various grains. 8,000 years ago, humans in Mesoamerica were cultivating corn, squash and beans. In Africa, the first crops included millet and watermelon. Humans first cultivated familiar plants that they had watched grow, recognized and understood. These plants were already a significant part of local diets prior to the innovation of agriculture, as you can see by the regional nature of plants used in each part of the world.

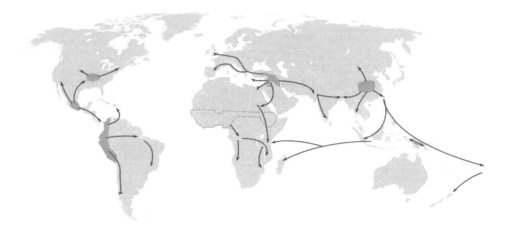

Animal Husbandry

The **domestication of animal species** was likely also a slow process, occurring around 8,000 years ago, as animals were first fenced in and tended in their natural grazing grounds, before they were moved closer to new human villages and communities. Local animals were domesticated, including goats and sheep in the Near East and water buffalo in Southeast Asia. In Mesoamerica, alpacas and llamas were domesticated. In Africa, animal domestication on a large scale came quite late, only after the introduction of cattle from South Asia.

Domestication has often failed, and a relatively few species of animals have been successfully domesticated for human use. With grain production, humans could feed livestock without grazing or supplement grazing and could use products from the livestock to enrich their own diets, the soil or to provide fiber.

Agriculture's Impact on Human Development

Almost at once, agriculture changed human lives and the human landscape. Nomadic human groups were small and typically lived in a way that offered little impact to the environment and world around them. Once humans settled in villages, they began, at once, exploiting their environment for resources, changing how they made their homes, and even altering their social structures. The forms of villages allowed people to make the best possible use of their space.

The first human settlements accompanied the beginning of agriculture. For the first time, human groups required settled communities with easily accessible, arable land. These villages developed in different ways at different times, depending upon the period and landscape.

The earliest villages were likely **nucleated** or **cluster villages**. A nucleated village has a cluster of homes, and in some communities, religious structures or other buildings, surrounded on all sides by farmland and pasture land. Archaeological excavations have shown building patterns of this sort throughout the ancient Near East, but they remain common in many parts of the world even today. **Linear villages** have an elongated shape, following a road or river. These are significantly less common.

During the Middle Ages, some villages were **walled**, with farmland included within the walls. **Round** villages are quite uncommon, but did occur in some Slavic countries. In these villages, homes and outbuildings surrounded a large area of pasture land for animals. **Grid-based village structures** were used in the Spanish colonies and remain the most popular choice for town planners today. Finally, **dispersed settlements** are uncommon in many parts of the world. These settlements lack traditional village structures, but are quite spread out. This is typical of some regions of North America.

The village provides space for homes, small kitchen gardens, and even small livestock in many cases. It does not include land use for larger-scale agricultural production, like growing grain. Land may be distributed in a variety of different ways, some still visible in the landscape today. In many parts of North America, land is visibly divided into large, square plots, while in parts of Europe, longer and narrower plots of agricultural land are more typical.

Shape, size and layout are all distinguishing features of a village, but not the only ones. Villages also reveal some distinct characteristics of changing human society. In villages, you can see buildings in different shapes and sizes, made of different materials and even placed differently within the village. These differences reflect social hierarchies. For instance, if all buildings in the village are made of wood, a building made of stone may reflect a higher status or a more important space.

Subsistence Agriculture

For many millennia, the majority of people worked to sustain their own lives, farming and producing food. Relatively few people could take up other occupations, as food production was highly labor intensive and time intensive. This is called **subsistence agriculture** and remains prevalent in the world today.

- In subsistence agriculture, most farmers produce only enough food to feed themselves, with relatively minimal excess to sell or save for future use.
- Subsistence farmers typically do not own the land they work. Land may be leased from a larger, non-farming landowner.
- Intensive, human or animal-powered methods are found in most subsistence farming communities.
- Other resources are also provided by the land or barter, with minimal use of cash. Homes may be built of locally available materials.

Subsistence agriculture is the most primitive form of agriculture, but does involve some use of simple management techniques. These become more complex as groups move toward an intermediate or transitional stage in the agricultural development process.

The following table shows three farming methods used in subsistence farming that may continue in transitional periods of agricultural development.

Slash and burn, also called swidden	Used to clear forests, the ash enriches soil. Common in the past, today this technique is associated with damaging farming practices in the rainforests of Central and South America.
Crop rotation	Another intermediate farming technique involving or planting different crops in fields in different years, allowing fields to lie fallow or choosing crops that provide specific nutrients to the soil.
Intertillage	Intertillage is a more intensive farming technique that allows a single field to produce a variety of crops within one season and spreads production throughout the season.

The Evolution of Agriculture

The transitional phase is sometimes called the **Second Agricultural Revolution**, with the first being the invention of agriculture. During the transitional phase, money economies became more important and many farmers began to grow enough to sell some surplus produce. New farming technologies, including fertilizers, become common, along with the seed drill.

During Europe's transitional period, new crops became accessible, including corn and potatoes. With more available crops, both food options and food production increased. A larger portion of society became devoted to employment or activities other than the production of food. In some regions, colonialism changed the nature of farming. Colonial powers forced modernization, but also improved irrigation, soil quality and provided options for loans for better equipment, seeds or other supplies.

The Von Thunen Model

Various models have been used to explain the development of agriculture and use of agricultural land. The most common is the Von **Thunen** model. According to Von Thunen, transportation plays a key role in land use. Developed in the early 19th century, Von Thunen's model is not applicable to subsistence farming or developed, modern farming, but does apply to transitional farming.

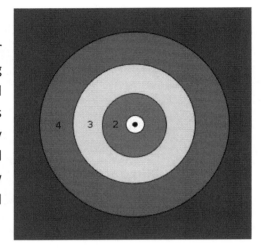

In this image, the black dot in the center represents a city. The narrow white ring around that city includes market gardens and dairy facilities. Market gardens produce fruits and vegetables, but do not grow grain. They are, in a more modern sense, what we would think of as small-scale gardening. The yellow ring produces grains and other field crops and the red livestock.

Variations on Von Thunen's theory distinguish between intensive livestock production and livestock ranching; however, the theory remains the same. This theory assumed several things:

1. Farmers transported goods via oxcart or similar. This theory predates the railways or any form of modern transportation.
2. Foods that are most perishable or most costly to transport are closest to the city center. Foods that are relatively light or easier to transport, like livestock, are situated further from the city center. Land too far from the city remains largely unused for agricultural purposes; however, subsistence farming might take place on this land.
3. Other forms of production might occur within some of these rings. For instance, timber production needs to be relatively near the city, due to the high costs of transport.

There are a number of weaknesses in Von Thunen's theory, even applied only to pre-industrial Europe. It assumes several things about the city and the farmers that may not be true in all circumstances: The assumptions are that:

- There are no geographic barriers, like mountains

- There are no other transportation options, like a river
- The city is isolated, without neighboring cities
- Land is equal in all areas, without differences in climate or soil
- The farmers always make the most logical and economically smart decisions with regard to food production.

Modern Farming

While the industrial revolution reduced the number of people involved in agriculture, agriculture remains the dominant human profession. The map above shows the world's arable land. Today, approximately 40 percent of the world's population continues to farm; however, only two million Americans are farmers. This contrast holds true in other economically developed states as well.

The **mechanization** of agriculture has had the greatest effect in economically developed regions. Commonly called **developed** or **modern farming**, this is distinguished from subsistence and intermediate farming. In these areas, mechanization, or the use of mechanical tools and machines in farming, has caused the following:

- Fewer people are involved in farming than in the past.
- Small family farms have been replaced by large, industrial farms.
- Food production continues to increase.

The transition from small-scale agriculture to commercial agriculture significantly changed the world over time, altering how we grow and eat our food. Commercial agriculture is common in developed regions of the world. Commercial agriculture required not only development in farming technology, but also significant changes in transportation technology. In order to replace many small farms throughout a state with fewer, larger, commercial farms, farmers must be able to transport goods much longer distances over time, without loss of food quality or spoilage. Some forms of technology, like food processing, have made a significant difference. Many foods can be frozen or canned for later use, making transportation in refrigerated trucks significantly easier. Fresh foods can also be transported with refrigeration, allowing foods grown quite far away to reach supermarkets in a town quickly, while they're still quite good to eat.

The commercialization of agriculture has allowed for improved specialization with regard to climate and land use, as well as increased accessibility. For instance, you can pick up oranges at any American grocery store. These oranges may well have been grown in Florida. You can't grow oranges in Iowa, but that's likely where your pork chops were produced.

Arable land can be devoted to crops, while less fertile soil often works well for ranching. Commercial agriculture extends beyond the developed world and into countries that are less economically developed. In these nations, commercial agriculture commonly takes the form of plantation agriculture. Plantation agriculture developed during the colonial period and continues, with massive farms producing goods like sugar, coffee and cocoa. This is cash crop production, designed for export. The crops are not used to feed the population of the state.

Changes in modern farming have brought about an improved food supply in many regions; however, other changes, sometimes called the **Green Revolution**, have led to reduced hunger. Higher yield crops, particularly rice, are key to this change. New varieties of basic grains, including rice, corn and wheat are more resistant to crop failures. While famines still exist around the world, they are less often the result of natural issues and more often the result of political ones. You should remember here that "green" does not refer to environmental benefits.

While modern technology has changed farming, reduced hunger and improved the yield of food crops, there are a number of controversies surrounding some or many aspects of modern farming, including the genetic modification of some food crops. These include:

- The environmental cost of large-scale farming is significant, in terms of water usage, pollution, the use of pesticides and the cost of transporting food long distances
- Concern over the safety and practices of genetic modification

- Issues with the ownership of seeds, since genetically modified crops are patented, unlike traditional seeds
- A concern with the fundamental unfairness of plantation systems has led to fair trade practices, buying direct from growers, and insuring the farmers are paid a fair wage for their labor

This is a response to the green revolution, and a growing number of farms are embracing different, more environmentally friendly practices. Consumers are seeking out foods produced locally, using fewer chemicals. It is critical to note that this reaction to the green revolution is a Western, economically developed phenomenon, and not of concern to much of the world's population; however, these are also the markets relying most heavily on large-scale farming.

Conclusions

The changes in agriculture are marked by progressive stages:

1. The First Agricultural Revolution marks the beginning of subsistence agriculture. Limited technology is employed, including the use of animals and human power to plow and work the fields. The domestication of plants preceded that of animals and subsistence agriculture continues in some parts of the world even today. The Agricultural Revolution led to a settled lifestyle and the creation of villages and larger communities.
2. The Second Agricultural Revolution included new tools, plants and soil treatments to improve soil production. This accompanied a changing economy and the ability of more of the population to engage in activities unrelated to food production. Pre-industrial revolution Europe is an example of a transitional agricultural economy.
3. The Third Agricultural Revolution marked the introduction of new technologies, new crops, and changes to extant crops. These increase crop stability, reduce low yields and have lowered famine. Additionally, transportation technology allows for more food production and for farmers to take advantage of the best climate and soil conditions for food production.
4. The Green Revolution questions modern agricultural practice, advocating an end to some aspects of the Third Agricultural Revolution and a return to locally produced food, with less environmental impact.
5. As you proceed, consider the impact of agriculture on how human groups use land, access resources and feed themselves.

Economic Development and Industrialization

Economic development is a key factor in human geography. We rely upon economic development as a way to categorize states, as a means of understanding political relations, and as a way of considering the quality of life and ways in which humans live in their environment. Often, during the course of your study, you'll see the terms "**more developed countries**" and "**less developed countries**". These terms have replaced the less-used "**first world**" and "**third world**".

Originally, the term first world referred to western democracies, the second world to isolated, communist states and the third world to less developed countries, particularly in Africa. A changing global world, including the end of the Soviet Union and Eastern Bloc, has altered the understanding and use of these terms. Today, countries are considered in comparison to one another using the broader, "more or less developed" terminology.

Simply defined, economic development is the growth of income and wealth. This is not personal economic development and wealth, as there are wealthy individuals in the poorest nations, but the wealth of the entire state as a whole. Some key points that can guide your analysis of economic development, and which will be covered in this chapter, include:

- Gross national product or GNP, per capita or per person
- Population growth
- Occupational structure of the work force
- Urbanization
- Consumption per capita
- Infrastructure
- Social conditions

Gross National Product

Gross national product, commonly written as GNP, is the total of all goods and services produced by corporations or citizens of a country in a given year. The GNP includes goods and services produced by a given nation outside of its borders. The **gross domestic product** is similar and may also be used as a measure of economic development, but measures only those goods and services within the country.

The per capita GNP is divided by the total population. Therefore, a small nation with a lower overall GNP might still have a much higher per capita GNP. This is only one measure of economic development; however, in broad terms, a nation that produces more goods and services per person is more economically developed than one that produces less. The map below illustrates the per capita GNP of various countries around the world.

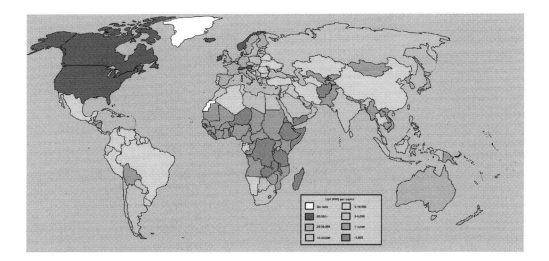

This map illustrates the significant differences in per capita GNP around the world. You can see the countries in dark blue and bright green have the highest per capita GNP. Those colored yellow, orange and pink have the lowest per capita GNP. Even at a glance the distribution is relatively unsurprising. Below, you can see a graphic showing the growth rate of per capita GNP over the 30-year period between 1980 and 2010. Green represents higher growth, and red represents lower growth.

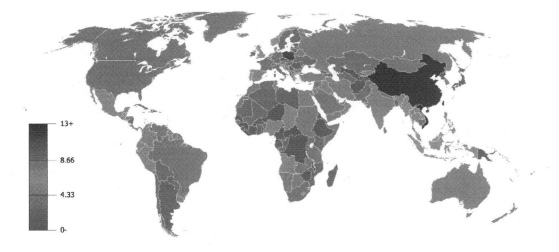

Here, you can see that some regions have experienced substantial growth, like China, while others have experienced very little or no change in GDP over this period. The majority of countries, including the United States and Russian Federation, show low to moderate growth. Countries with significant growth have undergone a period of economic development. These countries are becoming more, rather than less developed, according to this measure of growth.

Population Growth

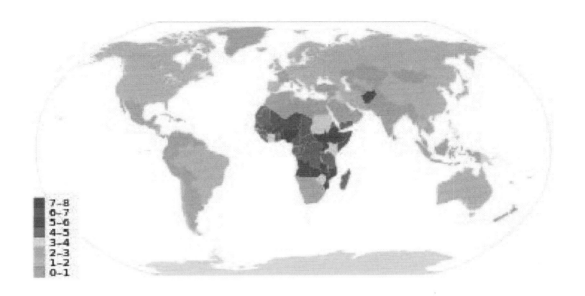

The map above illustrates fertility rates per woman, based on 2013 data. **Population growth** is another marker of economic development; however, lower population growth is correlated with higher economic development, as you can see by the image above. More economically developed nations show a fertility rate of fewer than three children per woman, while less economically developed nations show a much higher fertility rate. A higher population growth rate will result in a significant increase in population relatively quickly, even doubling population within a period of 70 years.

In states with high population growth, economic development will be significantly more difficult. A decrease in fertility rates is often accompanied by improved economic growth, better living conditions and a higher quality of life for citizens of a less developed state.

Occupational Structure of the Work or Labor Force

The occupational structure of the workforce can be divided into several categories. You should be aware of the three most important of these.

1. **Primary activities** take resources from the earth. These include farming of all sorts, mining and other activities. While these activities go on in all countries, in a less developed country, the majority of the population is employed in primary activities.
2. **Secondary activities** are manufacturing. For instance, lumber harvested by individuals involved in a primary activity might be made into paper by people working in a paper plant. This is an example of a secondary activity.
3. **Tertiary activities** perform services, like education, banking, retail or transportation. These activities do not produce material goods.

The more developed a nation, the more of the working population will work in tertiary fields. In a less developed country, the majority is employed in primary activities. In a developing country, secondary activities will become more important. For instance, in the United States, it is likely that many of the adults you know are, in some way, employed in tertiary fields. The study of human geography, for instance, is itself a tertiary field!

Urbanization

While we will discuss **urban development** at length later in this guide, you should understand that urbanization is a measure of development. The more of the population that lives in urban areas, here defined as communities of 2,500 people or more, the more developed the nation is. In less-developed countries, a larger percentage of the people live in cities. Looking at that measurement, you'll quickly see that even what we define as a small town in America is a "city". Less than half of the world's population lives in communities of more than 2,500 people today. Typically, more people living in larger communities is a sign of increased economic development.

Per Capita Consumption

This is a relatively broad heading, as consumption can refer to anything from fuel to food to consumer goods. Typically, as per capita income increases, consumption rises in concert. For instance, if you imagine the lifestyle of a subsistence rice farmer, he uses little in his day-to-day life. On the other hand, an urban professional uses significantly more resources of all kinds.

One-way consumption is often measured is by looking at CO2 emissions (also called greenhouse gas emissions.)The image below illustrates greenhouse gas emissions. As you can see, higher emissions are linked with more-developed countries.

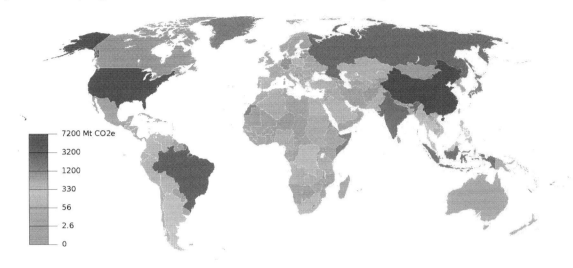

Infrastructure

Infrastructure is a broad term, including all of the things a society needs to function. Schools, roads, railways, airports, and hospitals are all part of infrastructure. A better infrastructure (or more of it) is a sign of a more-developed country. Less developed countries are less likely to have even basic infrastructure, including roads, access to utilities, and appropriate sanitation.

Adequate infrastructure is essential for a number of reasons. For instance, without access to appropriate sanitation, including clean water and toilet facilities, disease becomes much more common. Railways and roads allow both people and goods to move quickly and efficiently from place to place. In some areas, infrastructure is only in place in parts of the country, leaving others lacking key services.

Social Conditions

Social conditions are the final marker used to judge economic development. Some indicators of social conditions include:

- **Infant Mortality.** Less developed countries experience a higher rate of infant mortality. Various factors contribute to this, including a lack of prenatal care, a lack of access to pediatric health care, including vaccinations, inadequate food and a lack of clean water.

- **Life Expectancy.** This is lower in less developed countries. High infant mortality lowers life expectancy, as does a lack of health care and high rate of deaths in child birth.
- **Literacy.** High rates of literacy are expected in more developed countries, where all children have access to education. In less developed countries, many children do not have access to schools and may not have the opportunity to learn to read. Improved education is consistently linked to economic growth and development.
- **Health Care.** Health care is key to reduced infant mortality and increased life expectancy. In many less developed countries, access to health care is highly limited, with many people having no access to medical assistance at all.
- **Caloric Intake.** This directly relates to personal income and access to resources. Individuals in more developed nations are more likely to have an acceptable or high caloric intake than those in less developed countries.

The Human Development Index

As you can see, you need more than a single factor to effectively understand economic development in a given country. The United Nations relies upon the Human Development Index to combine these factors and create an easily understood rating of the development of different countries into different tiers. The Human Development Index includes the following criteria:

- Life expectancy
- Education, including adult literacy and enrollment in primary, secondary and tertiary education
- Real GNP per capita

The map on the next page illustrates the Human Development Index, according to the United Nations.

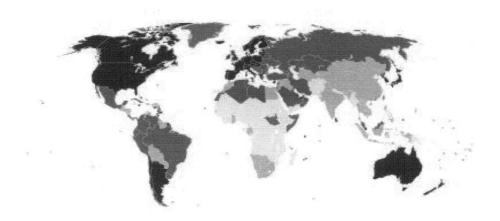

All models share a few key flaws. First and foremost, they only consider the **formal economy**. In many less-developed countries, both money and goods frequently change hands outside of the formal economy. These transactions are not recorded or taxed, but occur at small markets and elsewhere. These measures also do not consider any form of illegal economy, for instance, the drug trade, which may be impacting the economic development of the state.

Gender Inequality

Issues of gender inequality are a problem around the world, but especially in the developing world. In many countries, women lack the right to own property, divorce, or seek appropriate police protections against an abusive spouse. While women contribute economically around the world, often their contribution goes unrecognized and they lack control over their own economic destiny.

Health care issues have a strong impact on women's lives. A lack of appropriate maternal health care during pregnancy and birth leads to a high mortality rate. In areas with limited access to contraception, frequent pregnancy and childbearing limits women's economic potential and their ability to care for their children.

Gender preferences and inequalities have led to population issues in several countries, including India and China, as well as to domestic violence and murder. In India, these have led to high rates of gender-selective abortion and infanticide or killing of female infants. While this practice is illegal, it remains widespread in many areas.

In many countries, women still require a dowry to marry and daughters are considered less desirable than sons. Laws prohibiting dowries and infanticide are poorly enforced. In China, the one-child policy enforced for many years has led to the widespread abortion or abandonment of females. Dowry deaths, or murders when women's dowries are not paid, still exist in India, while in many Muslim regions, "honor killings" take women's lives if they are deemed to have morally dishonored their male relatives, such as through acts like premarital ex.

In many areas, women have less access to education than men, resulting in less economic opportunity and social power. In the West, women are increasingly seeking higher education and making progressive steps toward equality, but in the less developed world, girls are often working as children and are married quite young, further limiting their options. Early marriage is frightening, often non-consensual, and early motherhood comes with substantial health risks.

Gender disparity is a key factor in economic development and one which cannot be overlooked. Gender equality is, like economic development, measured in various ways, including the Gender Development Index.

Industrialization

Industrialization began with the industrial revolution in the 18th and 19th centuries. Industrialization dramatically altered the landscape of Europe. Prior to this time, most goods had been made by hand, in small workshops or cottage industries. Little machinery was used, and what machinery existed was simple and typically human or animal powered. A number of factors were essential for the creation of the industrial revolution in the late 18th century.

1. **Money**—in this case, wealth flowing into Europe, and England in particular, from its colonies.
2. The political, geographical and natural **resources** of England. The country was politically stable, somewhat isolated geographically and rich in resources, like coal and iron.
3. A willingness to invest time, energy and resources into new **inventions** and **innovations**.

The industrial revolution created the iron industry, led to the steam engine, trains and steam-powered ships. It moved people from the countryside to the cities and changed the way they lived their lives. Consumer goods became more accessible and affordable, and travel and movement became easier. The industrial revolution diffused throughout the world as new technology spread. Significant mining and manufacturing centers rose up in North America and Europe by the middle of the 19th century. Industrialization moved into Eastern Europe and Russia somewhat later.

Production methodologies have changed over time to increase efficiency and improve the quality of goods produced. In the early 20th century, Henry Ford invented **mass production** with the assembly line. Modern industrial practices have shifted and moved to increased **specialization**, in which a factory might produce a single part of a car, for instance, rather than building the car from start to finish as in the early automotive plants.

Even today, new industrial centers and centers of manufacturing are growing. Japan and more recently, China have become prominent industrial powers. Japan is particularly known for technological manufacturing, while China has worked to make itself an appealing center of industry for many different types of goods.

Theories of Industrialization

Several theories guide industrialization and the placement of factories for manufacturing. According to **Weber's** early 20th century model, published in The Theory of the Location of Industries, industry will grow in the lowest cost places, with three cost factors.

1. **Transportation**
2. **Labor**
3. **Deglomeration** and **agglomeration**

Other theorists built upon Weber, suggesting that factors were dependent upon similar industries and should be considered on an industry-by-industry basis. Increased profits and lower costs have led many industries to move out of higher cost areas, like the United States, and into lower cost ones, like China. This process is called **de-industrialization**.

Theories and Models of Development

There are a number of different **models of development**, each working with different assumptions about the process by which a state moves from a less developed to more developed economic state. Earlier in this text, we discussed Wallerstein's World Systems Theory. This theory explains economic development globally, but in this chapter we are primarily concerned with how development occurs within a particular country. You may wish to flip back and review Wallerstein's theory at this time, now that you've learned a bit more about economic development.

Rostow's Theory

Walt Rostow's theory of economic development, developed in the 1960s, remains in favor with many social scientists today. Rostow divided economic development into five distinct stages.

1. **Traditional or First Stage**
    a. Subsistence farming
    b. Resistance to change
    c. Rigid and unchanging social structure
2. **Preconditions for Take-off or Second Stage**
    a. Progressive leadership
    b. Commercialization of agriculture
    c. Improved infrastructure
    d. Greater flexibility
    e. Wider variety of goods manufactured
    f. Openness to new technology
3. **Take-off or the Third Stage**
    a. Industrial growth
    b. Urbanization
    c. Mass production
4. **Drive to Maturity**
    a. Spread of technology
    b. Specialized industry
    c. Introduction of international trade
    d. Reduced population growth
5. **Final Stage**
    a. Mass consumption of goods
    b. High incomes
    c. Majority of workers in tertiary jobs

Rostow's theory assumes that all states can reach a more developed state through a natural progression. Other models of modernization disagree.

Dependency Theory

Dependency theory suggests that more-developed nations act in ways that keep less-developed nations in a state of relative poverty. History, including the history of colonialism, has contributed to this. For dependency theorists, there is little hope of change in less-developed countries, as the political and economic actions of more developed countries prohibit economic growth and encourage continuing dependency on international aid.

Market-Based Model

A **market-based model** is a capitalist theory, based on the idea of the **free market economy**, with limited or no government controls. According to this theory, the existence of a free market will, eventually, lead to economic development. Property rights, in a modern and western context, are key to this development, as is the encouragement of a competitive market.

Challenges for Developing Countries

The different measures of economic development we have reviewed make many of the struggles of developing countries quite clear; however, there are a number of additional factors which may contribute to the overall poverty of many of the citizens of a developing nation. These include:

- **Political instability** and **corruption**. A lack of a stable government may increase violence, lessen access to international aid and limit the country's ability to join international trade organizations or partner with international corporations. A corrupt government is unlikely to invest funds into economic development or will invest those funds only for the good of the few, rather than the population as a whole.
- **Low social conditions** and **levels of social welfare** reduce the ability for economic growth. This is a self-fulfilling prophecy, as improvements often require economic growth. High rates of illness, high birth rates, low literacy and a lack of adequate health care and clean water reduce a country's ability to succeed and improve economically.
- **Debt to the World Bank**. The World Bank and **International Monetary Fund** exist to help less-developed nations with low-interest loans. Repayment of these loans typically requires economic reform, but those reforms are often not geared to improve the state of the country or its people.
- **Gender inequality**. As discussed above, in countries where women lack basic civil rights, economic development is typically much lower. Improved gender equality often goes hand-in-hand with economic development.

Economic realities impact all decisions, small and large, from both a personal perspective, a national one and an international one. As you can see, there are drastic differences between rich and poor countries around the world in terms of not only opportunity, but basic human needs. These differences dramatically impact how people live in their homes and in the places that they call home.

Urban Development

Urbanization is a recent development in human history. For much of our history, we lived in small communities, little more than family groups. With the introduction of agriculture, our communities grew to form villages and, eventually, some of those villages grew into towns and cities. One of the dividing factors between the village and the city is food production. In a village, all or nearly all residents are involved in food production. In a city, relatively few are involved in food production and most food is brought into the city from the surrounding countryside.

In the 20th century, urbanization progressed rapidly as more people moved from smaller communities to larger ones. Rates of urbanization differ between countries. In some areas, as much as 90 percent of the population lives in urban areas, while in others as little as 20 percent. Each nation defines a city differently; for instance, in the United States, a population of 2,500 is required, while in South Africa, only a population of 500 is required.

During the process of urbanization, people often move from rural areas to cities in search of better employment. Urban areas grow in two different ways. People migrate into cities and within the city and new residents typically experience a higher birth rate and population growth. This growth lowers as individuals find more stable employment over time and smaller families result. Cities are categorized in various ways, including by their population. It is important to realize that population counts for larger urban areas may be quite challenging or even inaccurate. A **primate city** dominates its nation and is a primary center of culture, growth, politics and economic development. Primate cities exist in both developed and less developed countries.

Theories of Urban Development

Historians, geographers and social scientists explain the development of cities in a variety of different ways. For the AP Human Geography test, you should be familiar with the following models of urban development or the creation of cities:

Hydraulic Civilization Model

The Hydraulic Civilization model, developed by **Karl Wittfogel**, attributes the creation of cities to improved irrigation. Better irrigation allowed for improved crop yields, lowering the total amount of labor required to produce enough food, and creating a food surplus. With the new irrigation system, increased social stratification, including a power elite, developed. The Hydraulic Civilization model does not apply to all parts of the world and provides no explanation as to the organization of or creation of irrigation systems.

Religious Models

Religious models, like those developed by **Paul Wheatley**, suggest that issues of faith and religion, rather than farming, spurred the development of urban areas. In early religions, the priests were actively involved in agriculture, providing them with significant social power. With the existence of social stratification on the basis of religion, cities developed as religious centers, created by the priest class within the society.

Multifactor Models

Many scholars rely upon multifactor models, believing that no single factor was responsible for the creation of cities. These included technical factors, like irrigation, religious ones and political ones. This explanation allows for regional variations, changes and even the social and political influence of other areas.

Diffusion Theory

Some scholars believe that cities sprung up organically for their own reasons, while others believe that the conditions to create a city are more unusual and therefore, many cities would have required the influence of others, or the **diffusion** of the ideas of urban development and the technology that influenced it. For **diffusionists**, cities in the Near East influenced those along the Nile River in Egypt and those in the Indus River Valley of India. Later, it becomes quite clear that urban development was the result of diffusion. For instance, as large empires developed, rulers created cities throughout their empires.

The First Cities

The first cities are often referred to as **cosmomagical cities**. Three characteristics distinguish these cities.

- The **city center** was typically marked by a large structure, like a temple, ziggurat or palace complex.
- Cities were laid out according to the **cardinal directions**, north, south, east and west.
- Cities were designed to meet **spiritual** and **religious needs** for order, and structured according to religious beliefs about the shape and design of the universe.

Early cities in many regions, including Asia, the Near East and Southeast Asia met these basic criteria. Early cities in Mesoamerica differed significantly and were typically larger in area, but lacked much of the technology found in other parts of the world, including metallurgy and the wheel.

While the first cities were largely religious in nature, later cities were much more functional. Ancient Greek cities included a religious center, the Acropolis, and a civic center, the Agora. Roman cities typically combined these two in the Forum, which served religious, political, social and trade functions.

Roman city design prevailed through much of Europe and the Mediterranean for several centuries; however, most Roman cities throughout Europe fell into decline after the fall of Rome, with cities only beginning to grow and thrive again during the early Middle Ages. While the Roman city was centered on the Forum, for the medieval city, the castle, cathedral and town walls were the most critical parts of the city. In much of Europe, the medieval city remains at the center of major cities, just as the Forum sits in the center of the city of Rome, even today.

Urban Design

In studying how cities look and function, we need to consider two key characteristics of the city. The first is **urban morphology**. Urban morphology is how the city is laid out, including roads, buildings, barriers, architecture and density. **Functional zoning** is the second aspect of urban design. Zoning dictates how different parts of the city function and what they are used for, ranging from industry to apartment complexes. These factors apply to both modern and ancient cities.

Consider the ways in which the different types of historical cities discussed above reflect morphology and zoning.

- The Roman Forum provided a place for various activities in one center. Palaces and large homes surrounded the forum, with smaller homes and apartments moving further away from the central area of town. The forum was the place in which the social elite conducted their affairs, not the average person.
- The medieval city was zoned into different areas, depending upon activities. Markets were typically located near the cathedral, while the castle, at the highest point, provided for defense. Members of different professions lived near one another, attended the same church and took their meals in the same inns. Some professions, like tanners, were pushed to the edges of the city walls for practical reasons. Since the cities were walled, buildings are

typically quite tall and narrow, and in some cases, built into the very walls of the town.

- Cities grew rapidly during and after the Renaissance. As power centralized in the 16th and 17th centuries, national capitals developed, providing a new source of central control from a single city center. By the late 18th and early 19th century, some of the cities underwent renovations to modernize them. These changed the city centers, but also pushed much of the population into outlying, overcrowded neighborhoods.
- In modern cities, zoning keeps industrial businesses out of residential neighborhoods, while urban morphology allows you to navigate the city. In most modern cities, a grid structure is favored, allowing you to move easily along roads that are clearly aligned in the cardinal directions. The division of cities continues today, creating a situation in which poor neighborhoods become poorer and rich ones richer.

Modern Urbanization

Modern cities solve some problems, but create many others. You need to understand both the benefits to the modern city and the problems with modern urbanization. Some of these benefits and problems are intrinsically linked. For instance, city-dwellers are less likely to rely on a personal vehicle for transportation; however, suburban sprawl leads to many people commuting some distance, commonly by car.

Possible benefits of cities include:

- City dwelling may have less environmental impact. City dwellers are less likely to drive, typically use less land and may use significantly less resources.
- It is easier to provide services, like education and healthcare, within a smaller geographical area, like a city.
- Urban areas support more diverse populations.
- Cities typically offer more job opportunities and more varieties of jobs.

Potential drawbacks of urban life include:

- Inner city struggles, including poverty, violence, poor access to decent housing and even a lack of access to grocery stores, medical facilities and other necessities.
- Suburban sprawl as people move from the city center outward, creating traffic difficulties, impacting farmland and altering or eliminating more rural communities.

Cities have been a part of our human landscape for many centuries and many of these problems existed even early on. The Romans worried about overcrowding and poor housing, and farmers in the Middle Ages complained about the city walls encroaching on their land.

The city has shaped our world and the places in it, creating capitals and centers of cultural life, religious sites and political ones. Cities have altered the land, shaping it to fit the needs of the people as they built, from Amsterdam in the flood plains of the Netherlands to island of Manhattan.

Practice Examinations

Sample Free-Response Answers

1. **Choose three early cultural hearths and describe the diffusion that occurred from each.**

High Scoring Response

Cultural hearths were centers of development, with technology, religion, and learning spreading outward from each through a process of expansion diffusion. The term cultural hearth refers particularly to the earliest cities, those created during or immediately after the First Agricultural Revolution and includes Mesopotamia, the Indus River Valley and Mesoamerica. These sites are not the founding sites of religion, but rather of culture in a broad sense.

Mesopotamia is one of several early centers of domestication, both of plants and animals. The people of early Mesopotamia built their villages out of air-dried mud bricks, beginning around 8000 BCE. Eventually, these early villages and towns evolved into cities, like Uruk, dating to 5500 to 4000 BCE and Nineveh, called cosmomagical cities, with a large ziggurat, or high-stepped pyramid at the center of the town. Not only did the people of early Mesopotamia learn how to cultivate crops, including types of barley and wheat, then livestock, like sheep and goats, eventually, they also developed intensive metalworking skills and the first systems of writing. The empires that developed in these early regions were lasting, well-organized and hierarchical.

In the Indus River Valley, early agricultural settlements spread cultivation technology and animal domestication throughout the valley. Early crops included wheat, barley and dates, beginning around 7000 BCE. The people of this region domesticated a number of local animal species, including a type of cattle, the zebu, dogs, cats, and possibly elephants. By 3000 BCE, a civilization had developed, including towns, like Mohenjo-Daro, dating to around 2600 BCE. Mohenjo-Daro was highly sophisticated, with a planned grid design, large citadel and extensive use of plumbing. The technology of Mohenjo-Daro and cities like it spread throughout the Indus River Valley. Artwork suggests the beginning of a strong religious tradition, incorporating a deity similar to the Hindu Vishnu.

The Mesoamerican cultural hearth is somewhat different than the other two. The Mesoamericans likely arrived around 13,000 BCE, with early agriculture and agricultural settlements dating to around 7000 BCE. Corn, the key crop of

Mesoamerica, was not domesticated until around 4000 BCE. While plant domestication occurred relatively early, the people of Mesoamerica did not domesticate large animals, like horses or cattle. Without large animals, they lacked some of the technology found elsewhere in the world, including the wheel. Cities developed significantly later in Mesoamerican history, around 1200 BCE. While cities came fairly late, they do show clear evidence of significant technology, including irrigation and large-scale building and sculpture.

While early cultures and cities varied, each influenced the language, architecture, culture, religion and technology of the surrounding region. Technology was created in response to local needs, from irrigation to metalworking to the wheel. Improved technology allowed, often, for better harvests and reduced farm labor for food production. Progressively, these changes allowed more people to live in cities.

Average Scoring Response

Cultural hearths are centers of culture and religion in the ancient world. These hearths led to the diffusion of agricultural and other practices throughout their region. Three of these hearths are Mesopotamia, the Yellow River Valley and the Nile River Valley. Agriculture developed in each of these regions, possibly independently of one another.

Along the Yellow River Valley of China, the first farmers cultivated rice and millet, working with stone tools. This is one of the few fertile regions of China, and over the length of the valley a number of different villages and communities developed. Cities came somewhat later, during the Shang dynasty around 1500 BCE. Iron working and pottery developed along the Yellow River, along with, eventually, written language.

In Mesopotamia, the first cities came significantly earlier than elsewhere, with cities appearing as early as 7500 BCE. These cities showed that agriculture had already developed enough to allow for a social hierarchy and specialized labor by this time. Farming and other forms of technology increased rapidly, allowing communities to grow and form new cities. Eventually, this led to a number of different empires in the Fertile Crescent, including the Assyrians and Babylonians, as well as to written language, accounting, extensive metalworking skill, the wheel and more.

Agriculture also developed along the Nile River Valley, in Egypt. Large villages existed by 3300 BCE and by 3100, the first united empire appeared, already able to compete with those in Mesopotamia. Egyptian culture spread and thrived, lasting into the Roman Empire.

All of these cultures grew up near river valleys, in the most fertile land available. This land offered excellent growing conditions and the most ample food supplies. The first cities grew from the first villages and towns, gradually increasing in size as the food supply allowed for a larger population. With more people came more opportunity for cultural diffusion, as technology, religion and political control spread.

Low Scoring Response

Cultural hearths are centers of culture and religion. Religions begin in cultural hearths, but so does new technology. There were seven cultural hearths. Three of those are Mesopotamia, Mecca, and Mesoamerica.

In Mesopotamia, agriculture developed fairly early, including wheat, barley, as well as sheep and goats. The use of animals provided more options for early farmers, including an ability to work the fields. With more food available, technology and eventually towns could develop. The development of cities and towns helped to spread technology and culture outward from the cities of Mesopotamia. Eventually, cultural diffusion from Mesopotamia may have helped initiate the development of agriculture in other regions.

Mecca is a religious hearth. Islam developed there and spread throughout the region relatively quickly, taking over much of the larger area within its first century. Islam changed the language, folk traditions, beliefs and cultural practices of the Arab people surprisingly quickly. Regulations about food usage also changed with the introduction of Islam.

In Mesoamerica, culture spread for many centuries without the introduction of cities. The Mesoamerican people began cultivating plants, but not grain. Grain, in the form of corn, came significantly later. The first cities did not develop until around 1200 BCE, with the Olmecs. The Olmecs preceded the great empires of Mesoamerica, like the Aztecs. The Mesoamericans did not have large pack animals, like oxen, so did all cultivation with human power.

2. **Gender disparities and inequalities impact social culture in significant ways. Explain at least three ways in which culture impacts the lives of women in the developing world.**

High Scoring Essay

In many less-developed societies and some more industrialized societies, women suffer significant discrimination solely on the basis of their gender. This discrimination takes many forms, from extremes, including murder, to regulations that limit their freedom, to limited access to health care, including family planning. Gender discrimination is measured on the Gender Discrimination Index or GDI. This includes a wide range of factors impacting women's lives and their well-being, as well as, in many cases, the well-being of their children.

While discrimination is a significant issues, in some cultures, female life is devalued to the extent that murder becomes an option. Traditionally, in India, a daughter's marriage requires a dowry. While dowries are no longer legal, the custom continues. When there is a dispute over dowry payments, brides are sometimes murdered, frequently with acid. In some Islamic countries, women deemed to have dishonored their families, typically through actions perceived as sexual impropriety, may be killed by their fathers or brothers to regain the family's honor. In one recent case, a Pakistani woman who had married without her father's approval was stoned in the street. While these cases involve adults, in countries that devalue female life, female infanticide and sex-selective abortion are also commonplace.

Cultural customs and laws that limit female freedoms reduce women's economic independence, limit their ability to choose their own relationships, and may leave them trapped in horrible situations. Even in developed countries, women may lack the ability to leave their homes without a male chaperone, to drive, or to attend university. In less-developed countries, that may extend to any form of education at all. Women who attempt to defy these norms often face not only social stigma, but even legal repercussions. Without education, women have few options, lack access to information and services, and cannot better their lives or those of their children.

Women's access to health care dramatically impacts their lives in a variety of ways. First and foremost, in parts of the less-developed world, access to contraception is limited, non-existent, or requires the support of the male partner. This eliminates any ability to control fertility. The risk of injury or death in childbirth is high, and access to prenatal care may be minimal. Particularly for teen mothers, birth is dangerous. A lack of prenatal care not only increases the risk to the mother, but also to the infant, leading to higher rates of infant mortality in less-developed nations. Repeated pregnancy and the burdens of child rearing reduce women's economic potential and further a cycle of poverty.

Economic development requires gender equality, or at least a reduced gender disparity. When women are able to control their own childbearing, they can improve their family's economic condition, reduce the risk of infant mortality and improve their own quality of life and social condition. Increased gender equality leads to lower birth rates, as women have fewer children and begin to have children later in life. Reduced population growth further supports overall economic development.

Average Scoring Essay

Gender disparities or the differences in the ways men and women live in the world can dramatically impact the quality of life and social conditions in a country in various ways. While gender equality has made significant progress in more –developed Western countries, this is not true in less-developed regions or even in some more-developed parts of the world. These gender disparities impact both women and children, infant mortality, economic well-being, and can even lead to population inequalities in terms of gender ratios.

A lack of status for women in the less-developed world typically leads to high rates of death in childbirth, high birth rates and high infant mortality, as well as early marriage. Early marriage, or marriage before the age of 18, leads to both a higher birth rate and a higher rate of complications in childbirth. Access to prenatal care is limited or non-existent. In some cultures, cultural taboos disallow appropriate medical treatment, and in others, health care is simply not available. Poor prenatal care is associated with poor pregnancy outcomes. This lack of health care and resources extends to infants, leading to increased infant mortality. Furthermore, when women cannot control the size of their families, they lack economic freedom, may have a limited ability to work, and often lack the ability to escape domestic violence or improve their situations.

When women and female children are devalued in society, they are more likely to become victims of infanticide or abandonment. In cultures, like India and China, that traditionally value male children far more than female, female newborns are far more likely to die than male newborns or to be left at orphanages. Furthermore, prenatal gender testing has led to high rates of sex-selective abortion, in which female fetuses are aborted. This is particularly true in China under the one-child policy. These cultural beliefs have created a significant population inequality, particularly in China. Today, China has more than 120 young men for every 100 young women.

Gender disparities can even lead to murder. In India, dowry killings still occur as the result of an unwillingness by a father to pay his daughter's dowry. These murders, typically covered-up as kitchen accidents, are illegal, but rarely prosecuted. The dowry custom also supports other forms of violence against women, including infanticide. In Islamic countries, honor killings are often tolerated. In these instances, when a woman has "dishonored" her family, perhaps by marrying a man they did not choose or even by being raped, she may be killed by her own parents, brothers or uncles.

In the west, gender equality issues are not life-or-death. They may be unfair or inconvenient, but lives are rarely at risk. In less-developed countries and those with strong cultural beliefs against women, that is far from true. From a high risk of death in childbirth and lack of access to family planning services to honor killings, the gender disparities in many parts of the world place women's lives and well-being at risk.

Low Scoring Essay

Gender differences are a significant factor in social condition. They can lead to murder, infanticide, and sex-selective abortion. In some cases, this results in population issues and other problems, particularly since there aren't enough women.

While domestic violence is responsible for many murders around the world, cultural issues may contribute in some areas. In Muslim regions, particularly fundamentalist countries, women who violate social rules around sex may be murdered for dishonoring their families or may even be sentenced to death by the courts. Women are also killed for the same reason in India.

Infanticide, or the killing of young infants, impacts female children far more than male, particularly in India and China. In China, traditional customs favor male children and the communist government's one-child law has led to extensive female infanticide, as well as abandonment. Many families did not care for, directly killed or left female children at orphanages so they could go on to have a male child. In India, traditionally male children are also preferred and female children considered a burden. Again, abandonment or direct infanticide is relatively common to avoid raising an unwanted female child.

Sex-selective abortion is the practice of terminating a pregnancy after testing reveals the gender of the fetus. While illegal in India, the practice continues. In China, high rates of abortion accompanied the one-child policy, but female fetuses were more likely to be aborted. This has led to a generation of men without female partners, since there are so few available women. Population inequality is likely to further reduce the Chinese population, since there is a lower number of fertile women available.

These factors are the result of gender inequality. If women were valued as people, they would not be murdered and female children would be as desirable as male children.

Practice Quiz 1

Multiple-Choice

1. Which of the following distorts a map to illustrate population differences?
   a. A cartograph
   b. A cartogram
   c. A dot map
   d. A Robinson projection

2. Which of the following is an example of a cosmomagical city?
   a. Beijing
   b. Washington D.C.
   c. Rome
   d. Athens

3. Suburban sprawl is an example of:
   a. Urban development
   b. Economic development
   c. Agricultural development
   d. Industrialization

4. Which of the following would you expect NOT to find in a less developed country?
   a. Gender equality
   b. High birth rate
   c. Low life expectancy
   d. Low literacy rate

5. In which of the following countries would literacy be lowest?
   a. France
   b. India
   c. Poland
   d. Canada

6. Which farming technique is associated with subsistence farming?
   a. Slash and burn
   b. Seed drills
   c. Mechanized farming
   d. Commercial farming

7. In which of the following countries did the industrial revolution begin?
    a. France
    b. Germany
    c. The United States
    d. England

8. A Robinson projection:
    a. Distorts shape
    b. Distorts size
    c. Distorts positions
    d. Distorts all of the above, but to a minimal degree

9. Which provides the most accurate representation of the earth?
    a. Robinson projection
    b. Mercator projection
    c. Globe
    d. Map

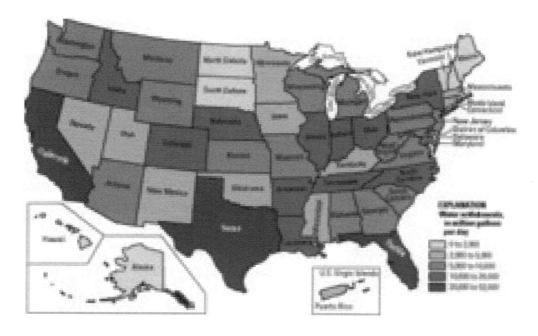

10. The map above is an example of:
    a. Thematic map
    b. Isoline map
    c. Robinson projection
    d. Choropleth map

11. **What is the function of the U.S. Census?**
    a. To review economic data
    b. To improve economic conditions
    c. To count the population
    d. To assign seats on the U.S. Senate

12. **Which of the following is a characteristic of infant mortality in the United States?**
    a. It is the lowest in the world.
    b. It is higher than expected for a developed country.
    c. It is the highest in the world.
    d. It is increasing

13. **Which of the following would you expect to have the lowest infant mortality rate?**
    a. Singapore
    b. The United States
    c. Canada
    d. Iceland

14. **How might a government impact or change population growth to meet goals?**
    a. Restrictive policies
    b. Expansive policies
    c. Eugenics
    d. All of the above

15. **Which of the following has the most restrictive population policies?**
    a. China
    b. Singapore
    c. India
    d. Italy

16. **Which of the following is an example of a push factor?**
    a. Job growth
    b. Good agricultural conditions
    c. Economic recession
    d. Cultural tolerance

17. Which is a characteristic of immigrants?
  a. They are older, with families
  b. They move from urban areas
  c. They move to rural areas
  d. They move into urban areas

18. Which of the following periods saw the highest levels of immigration to the United States?
  a. The 1950s
  b. The 1940s
  c. The 1980s
  d. The 1920s

19. Which disease are you most likely to see in a less-developed country?
  a. Alzheimer's
  b. Cancer
  c. Cholera
  d. Diabetes

20. In which of the following countries have women been killed over dowry disputes?
  a. Canada
  b. India
  c. China
  d. Russia

21. Isolationism is characteristic of which of the following policies?
  a. During the 1930s, the United States refused to become involved in European politics.
  b. During the 18th century, huge numbers of Africans were forcibly moved by slavers to colonies in North, Central and South America.
  c. Trade agreements have helped to increase the economic development in some countries.
  d. During the 19th century, Great Britain held power over much of the world through active colonialism.

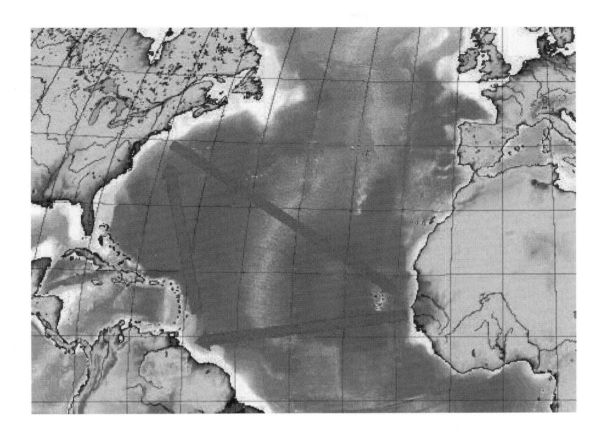

22. The map shown here illustrates:

    e. Patterns of voluntary emigration

    f. Patterns of forced migration

    g. Patterns of refugee movements

    h. Water currents

23. A pull factor is:

    a. A reason to leave a place

    b. A reason to move to a place

    c. A reason to flee a place

    d. An consideration in economic development

24. The Green Revolution describes:

    a. A move away from commercial agriculture

    b. A desire for political change

    c. Fair trade practices

    d. Higher yield food production

25. In which of the following places might you find plantation agriculture?
   a. Brazil
   b. France
   c. The United States
   d. Mexico

26. Which of the following is an example of material culture?
   a. Pop music
   b. Traditional stories
   c. Myths
   d. Denim jeans

27. English is an example of:
   a. An Anglican language
   b. A Romance language
   c. A Latin language
   d. A Germanic language

28. If two people speak dialects of the same language:
   a. They will communicate relatively easily
   b. They cannot communicate
   c. They will communicate, but with misunderstanding and difficulty
   d. Only the accent with differentiate the dialects

29. Which of the following languages are most closely related?
   a. French, German and Dutch
   b. French, Spanish and Italian
   c. Romanian, German, Ukrainian
   d. Russian, Ukrainian, Hindi

30. Belief in Shiva is part of:
   a. Hinduism
   b. Judaism
   c. Buddhism
   d. Confucianism

31. Sacred sites of what religion are found in Jerusalem?

    a. Christianity

    b. Judaism

    c. Islam

    d. All of the above

32. The Ganges River is sacred to believers of what religion?

    a. Hinduism'

    b. Christianity

    c. Buddhism

    d. Judaism

33. Which is an example of relocation diffusion?

    a. The spread of pop music

    b. Modern fashion movements inspired by hip-hop

    c. The game of cricket, played in India

    d. Chinese take-out

34. The Hajj is:

    a. A religious pilgrimage in Islam

    b. Prayer requirements in Islam

    c. Fasting for Ramadan

    d. Donation to charity in Islam

35. Which is the best definition of proselytization?

    a. A set of strongly held religious beliefs

    b. A desire to share beliefs and convert non- believers

    c. The belief that a personally held religion is the correct one

    d. Intolerance of other religious beliefs

36. The Great Wall of China is an example of:

    a. A superimposed boundary

    b. A delimitation

    c. A demarcation

    d. A religious structure

37. Which of the following is an exclave?

a. Alaska

b. Quebec

c. The Vatican

d. Hawaii

38. Who developed the Rimlands Theory?

a. Mahan

b. Spykman

c. Wallerstein

d. Mahan

39. What innovation made the Heartland Theory irrelevant and inaccurate?

a. Steam travel

b. Railways

c. Air travel

d. The nuclear bomb

40. When did many African states join the United Nations?

a. The 1950s

b. The 1960s

c. The 1970s

d. The 1980s

41. Pop culture commonly spreads through:

a. Relocation diffusion

b. Hierarchical diffusion

c. Contagious diffusion

d. Stimulus diffusion

42. In which of the following countries has an ethnic genocide occurred?

a. South Africa

b. Syria

c. Israel

d. Rwanda

43. Gerrymandering is:
   a. Redrawing political borders for political gain
   b. Redrawing international borders
   c. Assigning lands after a war
   d. A diplomatic tactic

44. Which agricultural products were produced closest to the city center in pre-industrial Europe?
   a. Grain
   b. Meat
   c. Dairy
   d. Dairy and vegetables

45. What organization makes laws regarding the use of international waters?
   a. NATO
   b. The Warsaw Pact
   c. The United Nations
   d. The EU

46. Refugees typically flee their countries due to:
   a. Push factors
   b. Pull factors
   c. Violence and persecution
   d. Economic conditions

47. Indo-European and Amerindian language families are represented on what continent?
   a. North America
   b. South America
   c. Europe
   d. Both North and South America

48. Which of the following is not an Indo-European language?
   a. Hindi
   b. Romanian
   c. Navajo
   d. English

49. Core and periphery are terms connected to:
   a. World banking theory
   b. World markets theory
   c. World systems theory
   d. World economy theory

50. Which of the following states is currently experiencing devolution?
   a. France
   b. The United States
   c. Great Britain
   d. India

51. A river divides two states. This is an example of a(n):
   a. Geometric boundary
   b. Physical boundary
   c. Superimposed boundary
   d. Antecedent boundary

52. Which of the following theorists influenced the ideology of the Nazi party?
   a. Mahan
   b. Wallerstein
   c. Ratzel
   d. Mackinder

53. Villages developed:
   a. During the first agricultural revolution
   b. During the second agricultural revolution
   c. During the third agricultural revolution
   d. During the green revolution

54. The cities of Europe declined rapidly:
   a. After the Crusades
   b. During the Middle Ages
   c. After the Fall of Rome
   d. During the 18th century

55. Which of the following makes it difficult to accurately calculate economic activity in some countries?

a. The formal economy
b. Taxation
c. Barter
d. The informal economy

56. Which of the following suggests that less developed countries are unlikely to become more developed?

a. The World Bank
b. The International Monetary Fund
c. Dependency Theory
d. The World Systems Theory

57. Islands of development or special economic zones are designed to:

a. Improve conditions for residents
b. Encourage foreign investment
c. Provide space for local entrepreneurs
d. Pay off foreign debt

58. In a less-developed country, tourism:

a. Provides needed jobs
b. May exploit the people and environment
c. Improves conditions in the country
d. Reduces environmental damage

59. Which is an example of a primate city?

a. Rio de Janeiro
b. Chicago
c. Rome
d. Baghdad

60. Where are you most likely to find dispersed settlements?

a. The American Midwest
b. Central Europe
c. Western Europe
d. The American Northeast

61. Fair trade products are:
   a. Grown organically
   b. Grown on plantations
   c. Grown in Central America
   d. Sold directly by the grower at a fair price

62. Corn grown in the United States is used for:
   a. Food
   b. Livestock feed
   c. Fuel
   d. All of the above

63. What innovation has allowed food to be grown further from its final destination?
   a. Refrigerated transportation
   b. Better fertilizer
   c. Mechanization
   d. High-yield seeds

64. Gentrification is best defined as:
   a. Improving lower-class neighborhoods for the benefit of the residents
   b. Rebuilding lower-class neighborhoods to increase their desirability
   c. Publically-funded housing projects
   d. Voluntary segregation

65. Inner city neighborhoods:
   a. May lack essential services
   b. May experience voluntary segregation
   c. Are prone to a higher crime rate
   d. All of the above

66. Which of the following was a strong contributing factor to the success of the industrial revolution?
   a. The train
   b. The steam engine
   c. The spinning jenny
   d. Labor laws

67. Spanish colonial towns in Central and South America use which structure?
a. Grid
b. Central
c. Elongated
d. Rondel

68. Zoning:
a. Controls the social hierarchy within the city
b. Controls what type of buildings and functions occur where
c. Controls how the city is laid out
d. Provides adequate space for lower-income neighborhoods

69. The function of the World Bank is:
a. To support the global economy
b. To loan money to developing countries
c. To help improve the social conditions of individuals in developing countries
d. To assist companies investing in less developed countries

70. The terms First, Second and Third World used to be favored by human geographers. What was the Second World?
a. Less-developed countries
b. Pre-industrial countries
c. Western democracies
d. Communist countries

71. Which three factors did Weber's theory of least cost include:
a. Labor, transportation, raw materials
b. Labor, transportation, deglomeration
c. Labor, transportation, agglomeration
d. Agglomeration, transportation, land

72. Mass production was created by:
a. British spinning mills
b. Henry Ford
c. The steam engine
d. The industrial revolution

73. Tertiary jobs are:

    a. Related to agricultural production

    b. Related to manufacturing

    c. Related to the service industry

    d. All of the above

74. Which of the following is NOT a goal of the World Health Organization?

    a. Increased vaccination rates

    b. Improved maternal and child health

    c. Clean water supplies

    d. Increase birth rates

75. Which of the following is likely to allow information to spread quickly from person-to-person in the world today?

    a. Radio

    b. Television

    c. Music

    d. The Internet

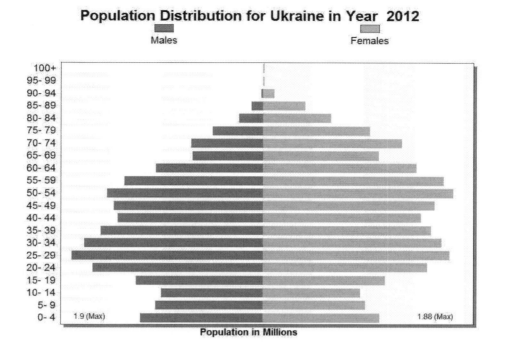

Population Distribution for Ukraine in Year 2012

Males   Females

1. This population pyramid provides information about the Ukrainian population as of 2012. Using what you know about human geography and population demographics, respond to this population pyramid.

   Include a discussion of the following, at minimum:

   - Birth and death rates
   - Population demographics
   - Dependency ratio
   - Gender disparities

2. Describe push and pull factors influencing European immigration to the United States in the 19th and early 20th century. Include at least three push factors and three pull factors that led to high rates of immigration during this period.

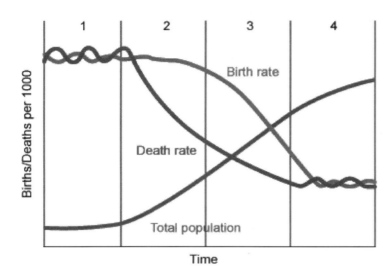

3. The Demographic Transition Model is a useful tool for human geographers; however, it is not always applicable. Explain at least three ways in which the Demographic Transition Model fails to accurately predict population growth or decline.

Practice Quiz 2

Multiple-Choice

1. **Which of the following is the most important religious holiday in Judaism?**
   a. Hanukah
   b. Passover
   c. Yom Kippur
   d. Rosh Hashanah

2. **What is a lingua franca?**
   a. A language related to French
   b. A language used in a colonial region
   c. A language commonly taught and understood
   d. A language that is particularly hard to understand

3. **Which of the following countries uses only a single language?**
   a. Denmark
   b. Mexico
   c. Switzerland
   d. The United States

4. **A dot map is used:**
   a. To show distributions
   b. To show environmental features
   c. To illustrate resource usage
   d. To show population

5. **GPS determines latitude in relation to ___ and longitude in relation to ___:**
   a. The equator, Antarctica
   b. The prime meridian, equator
   c. The equator, prime meridian
   d. The equator, Greenwich mean

6. **Geographic information systems are:**
   a. Paper maps
   b. Computer systems that combine various geographic data
   c. A computer program that relies on GPS data
   d. Measures to record elevation

7. **Which of the following is a cultural hearth for religion?**
    a. Jerusalem
    b. Chicago
    c. Paris
    d. Naples

8. **At what point in time would you expect cartography to become more accurate:**
    a. After 500 CE
    b. After 1500 CE
    c. After 1800 CE
    d. After 1600 CE

9. **Which of the following is the least advantageous?**
    a. A landlocked state
    b. A compact state
    c. An elongated state
    d. A prorupted state

10. **The Demographic Transition model suggests:**
    a. Birth rates will fall with development
    b. Birth rates will increase with development
    c. Life expectancy will decrease with development
    d. Life expectancy will be unchanged with development

11. **Which of the following typically measures social conditions and economic development?**
    a. The GNP
    b. The GDP
    c. The HDI
    d. The GDI

12. **Infrastructure describes:**
    a. Natural features of the environment
    b. Political structures of the state
    c. The use of land
    d. Roads, bridges, utilities and ports

13. **The region shares a language, culture and strong identity. These are all:**
    a. Centripetal forces
    b. Centrifugal forces
    c. Push factors
    d. Pull factors

14. **Which is an example of commercial agriculture?**
    a. A family farm with 15 cattle that sells milk and cheese at a local market
    b. A rice farmer planting rice by hand
    c. A large cattle ranch in Texas
    d. An organic farm producing a variety of vegetables, worked by members of the community

15. **Which are you likely to find in a semi-arid climate?**
    a. A dairy
    b. Grain production
    c. Rice production
    d. Ranching

16. **According to Thomas Malthus:**
    a. Food production would exceed population growth
    b. Population growth would exceed food production
    c. Food production would match population growth
    d. Population would increase arithmetically and food production geometrically

17. **In a village in England in the 16ᵗʰ century, you might expect to find homes built from:**
    a. Mud bricks
    b. Stone
    c. Wattle
    d. Stucco

18. Walled villages and cities are closely associated with:
   a. The ancient Near East
   b. Ancient Greece
   c. Medieval Europe
   d. Modern Europe

19. In a nucleated village, higher-status activities are:
   a. Located closer to the outskirts of the village
   b. Located in particular zones
   c. Located closer to the center of the village
   d. Located outside the village

20. In a round village, pastures are:
   a. On the outskirts of the village
   b. Behind each home or dwelling
   c. In the center of the village, surrounded by homes
   d. In the hills outside the village

21. According to Von Thunen's theory, which types of food are furthest from the city center?
   a. Livestock butchering
   b. Vegetable gardens
   c. Grain production
   d. Ranching

22. How long ago did plant domestication first occur?
   a. 7,000 years ago
   b. 8,000 years ago
   c. 10,000 years ago
   d. 12,000 years ago

23. Languages became more standardized following what?
   a. The discovery of the Americas
   b. World War I
   c. The Industrial Revolution
   d. The invention of the printing press

24. Literacy is a typical marker of:
   a. Social condition
   b. Technology
   c. Religion
   d. Culture

25. Which of the following is an example of folk or traditional culture?
   a. Maria's family makes tamales for Christmas, using her great-grandmother's recipe
   b. Jill's family has pizza on Friday nights
   c. Ben is excited to attend his first pop concert
   d. Anna was the first in her family to attend a university

26. Which of the following is considered a lingua franca today?
   a. English
   b. French
   c. Japanese
   d. Mandarin Chinese

27. Which of these world religions is the oldest?
   a. Buddhism
   b. Christianity
   c. Islam
   d. Hinduism

28. Which of the following is a trait linked to animism?
   a. Belief in a single god
   b. Belief in multiple gods
   c. Belief in a single religious founder
   d. Belief in spirits in all things

29. What are the two different branches of Islam?
   a. Orthodox and Reform
   b. Sunni and Reform
   c. Shiite and Sunni
   d. Shiite and Orthodox

30. According to World Systems Theory, the United States is an example of:
    a. A Core country
    b. A peripheral country
    c. A less developed country
    d. A more developed country

31. According to Rostow's developmental model, which stage is the most resistant to change?
    a. The First
    b. The Second
    c. The Third
    d. The Fifth

32. In the United States, how are raw materials for manufacturing most commonly transported?
    a. Ship
    b. Train
    c. Truck
    d. Air

33. Many states in the southwestern United States are defined by:
    a. Geographical boundaries
    b. Geometric boundaries
    c. Physical boundaries
    d. Lines of demarcation

34. A stateless nation lacks:
    a. A national identity
    b. A culture
    c. A population
    d. A territory

35. Which of the following political systems combines religion and politics in government?
    a. Monarchy
    b. Democracy
    c. Dictatorship
    d. Theocracy

36. State boundaries include:
   a. Only the land
   b. Land and subterranean resources
   c. Land and water
   d. Land, resources, water and air

37. The United Nations is the most powerful supranational organization today. It was preceded by another organization, created after World War I:
   a. NATO
   b. The Warsaw Pact
   c. The EU
   d. The League of Nations

38. Which of these world religion's is growing the fastest today?
   a. Islam
   b. Christianity
   c. Hinduism
   d. Buddhism

39. Which of the following regions is most likely to identify as non-religious?
   a. The Southern United States
   b. Western Europe
   c. India
   d. Saudi Arabia

40. Which of the following is landlocked?
   a. Japan
   b. The United States
   c. Switzerland
   d. The United Kingdom

41. Which of the following countries is most likely to devolve in the near future?
   a. Canada
   b. Belgium
   c. Switzerland
   d. France

42. Which of the following does NOT have a low birth rate?

a. Canada

b. Australia

c. France

d. Nigeria

43. In a city, land value is highest:

a. In the central business district

b. In gentrified neighborhoods

c. In commercialized areas

d. In the suburbs

44. Dependency ratios consider:

a. How many people are ill

b. How many people are above age 64

c. How many people are under 15

d. How many people are under 15 or above 64

45. Which of the following countries is an example of a theocracy?

a. Iraq

b. India

c. Israel

d. Iran

46. Space-time compression refers to:

a. Modern communication technology

b. Modern travel technology

c. Economic globalization

d. All of the above

47. High infant mortality is connected to:

a. Improving social conditions

b. High birth rates

c. Low birth rates

d. High life expectancy

48. Which is the best definition of desertification?
   a. Intentional creation of arid land
   b. Progressive loss of adequate water in semi-arid areas
   c. Leaving rural areas for urban ones
   d. Leaving the inner city for the suburbs

49. Which of the following countries is experiencing a gender disparity in population as a result of population control policies?
   a. Nigeria
   b. Saudi Arabia
   c. China
   d. Singapore

50. Which is the most likely to produce distinct linguistic differences?
   a. A flat country
   b. Rivers
   c. Large mountain ranges
   d. All of the above

51. What factor is leading to a growing decline in life expectancy in many African countries?
   a. Infant mortality
   b. Death in childbirth
   c. AIDS
   d. Political instability

52. Boundary disputes over natural resources are:
   a. Definitional
   b. Allocational
   c. Operational
   d. Functional

53. Which of the following is an NOT example of a fragmented country?
   a. Austria
   b. The United Kingdom
   c. The United States
   d. New Zealand

54. Popular culture is linked to:
   a. Isolation
   b. Regional differences
   c. Cultural diffusion
   d. Relocation diffusion

55. Which is the most common Sino-Tibetan language?
   a. Mandarin Chinese
   b. Cantonese
   c. Thai
   d. Japanese

56. Choose the best definition of an edge city?
   a. A suburb with housing outside of a city
   b. A residential area with various services, including shopping and health care outside the city center
   c. A tenement on the outskirts of a city
   d. A community absorbed into a larger city

57. John lives in a loft downtown, converted from an old industrial building. His neighborhood is home to a number of small businesses. John's neighborhood is:
   a. An edge city
   b. A suburb
   c. Gentrified
   d. Agglomerated

58. Which of the following describes a special economic zone?
   a. A region with access to inexpensive labor, tax breaks and other incentives
   b. A tourist zone with commercialized sites and activities
   c. An area in need of international assistance
   d. An area in need of revitalization and investment

59. Choose the explanation that describes voluntary segregation.
   a. Jim Crowe laws in the American South.
   b. Apartheid in South Africa
   c. Chinatown in San Francisco
   d. All of the above

60. What conflict in Europe led to large numbers of refugees?
   a. The fall of communism in Romania
   b. The change of government in Poland
   c. The fall of the Berlin wall
   d. The conflict in Yugoslavia in the early 1990s

61. The Warsaw Pact was a supranational organization created in response to:
   a. NATO
   b. The United Nations
   c. The European Union
   d. The League of Nations

62. Which of the following is a significant epidemic in the world today?
   a. Tuberculosis
   b. Smallpox
   c. Polio
   d. AIDS

63. Illnesses transmitted from person-to-person are:
   a. Vector-borne illnesses
   b. Epidemics
   c. Contagious
   d. Endemic

64. Which is an example of vector-borne illness?
   a. Cholera
   b. Malaria
   c. AIDS
   d. Tuberculosis

65. Choose the best definition of sovereignty.
   a. The authority of a state to govern itself
   b. Legally holding land or territory
   c. Recognition by other states and supranational organizations
   d. Defined borders

66. Sharecropping or indentured servitude are more likely to be found in:
   a. Ranches
   b. Plantation agriculture
   c. Fair trade farms
   d. More developed countries

67. Which of the following factors contributed to the fall of the Soviet Union and Eastern Europe?
   a. Race
   b. Ethnicity
   c. Literacy
   d. Religion

68. Ethnic cleansing is:
   a. An attempt to eliminate an entire ethnicity from a state or region, commonly through violence
   b. An attempt to change the practices of a given ethnicity
   c. Acts of violence against members of a particular ethnicity
   d. Forced migration of members of an ethnicity, without violence

69. In a federal government, individual states or provinces within a country:
   a. Lack power
   b. Hold power only at the will of the state
   c. Have power independent of the state, but with some restrictions
   d. Have sovereignty

70. Jill works in a small local grocery store, selling a variety of organic foods. She is involved in:
   a. Primary industry
   b. Secondary industry
   c. Tertiary industry
   d. None of the above

71. Which factor is key to Von Thunen's theory of agricultural distribution?

    a. Cost

    b. Transportation

    c. Labor

    d. Agglomeration

72. Per capita means:

    a. Overall

    b. Per mile

    c. Per person

    d. Per working adult

73. Pidgin languages are:

    a. Formally written languages

    b. Casually used languages combining elements of two different languages

    c. Trade languages

    d. Lingua franca

74. Which of the following might be the reason for a nation's choice of an official language?

    a. The state is monolingual

    b. The language is neutral, avoiding favoring one group or another

    c. The language is the most commonly spoken

    d. All of the above

75. A state that believes in secularism:

    a. Has a state religion

    b. Supports separation of church and state

    c. Bans religion

    d. Supports atheism

Free-Response Questions

1. Explain one current religious conflict in the world today. Include the following:
   - A brief history of the conflict
   - How the conflict relates to place
   - How the conflict relates to political organization and control

2. Introduce three different geopolitical theories and explain how each has impacted the history of the 20th or 21st centuries.

3. Choose one megacity and discuss its development. The city you choose may be in the developed or less-developed regions of the world and can be megacity, world city or primate city.

Practice Quiz 3

Multiple-Choice

1. **Which of the following occurs during the "Drive to Maturity", according to Rostow?**
   a. Manufacturing sector develops
   b. Agriculture improves
   c. Development of wider industrial base
   d. Static society

2. **Who developed the Central Place Theory?**
   a. Rostow
   b. Mahan
   c. Christaller
   d. Wallerstein

3. **Which of the following describes absolute location?**
   a. Position in relation to state borders
   b. Position within the state
   c. Geographic coordinates
   d. Position in relation to other states

4. **Internal physical and cultural characteristics of a place are:**
   a. Site
   b. Location
   c. Situation
   d. Place

5. **What is the function of the Demographic Transition Model?**
   a. It predicts population growth.
   b. It compares population and food supply
   c. It considers population in relation to development of society
   d. It measures population in relation to the environment

6. **What does the Gall-Peters projection distort?**
   a. Size
   b. Shape
   c. Position
   d. All traits to a lesser extent

7. **Choose the best definition of a cognitive or mental map.**
    a. A cognitive map has minimal distortion.
    b. A cognitive map is drawn from memory without reliance on geographical data.
    c. A cognitive map includes information about human populations.
    d. A cognitive map provides comprehensive information about places.

8. **If you need to study the relative elevation of various places, which type of map would you use?**
    a. Thematic map
    b. Isoline map
    c. Choropleth map
    d. Robinson Projection

9. **What percentage of the overall human population lives in cities?**
    a. 40
    b. 50
    c. 60
    d. 70

10. **Which two countries have populations of more than one billion?**
    a. India and Pakistan
    b. China and Pakistan
    c. China and the U.S.
    d. China and India

11. **Choose the best definition of physiological density?**
    a. Number of people per square mile or kilometer
    b. Number of people per unit of arable land
    c. Number of people per province or state
    d. Number of farmers per unit of arable land

12. **Which of the following factors impact carrying capacity?**
    a. Climate, technology, wealth, access to resources
    b. Climate, arable land, wealth
    c. Climate, population, arable land, wealth
    d. Population, land, climate, technology

13. If a population pyramid is top-heavy, this indicates:
  a. More young people
  b. More working people
  c. More old people
  d. A larger overall population

14. What does the crude birth rate measure?
  a. The number of women of fertile age
  b. The number of live births per 1,000 people per year
  c. The number of pregnancies per 1,000 people per year
  d. The number of live births per year

15. What numbers indicate "replacement level fertility"?
  a. 2-2.5
  b. 2.1-2.5
  c. 2.5-2.7
  d. 2.3-2.5

16. Which of the following led to a large refugee crisis in Europe?
  a. The Balkan Wars
  b. The fall of the Soviet Union
  c. The Vietnam War
  d. The Khmer Rouge

17. Immigration to the U.S. was first restricted in:
  a. 1918
  b. 1914
  c. 1921
  d. 1945

18. The term "brain drain" refers to:
  a. Lack of educational opportunities
  b. Educated individuals migrating away from their original homes
  c. Increased educational opportunity in the city
  d. Reduced educational opportunity in the inner city

19. The phrase "activity space" describes:
   a. Temporary moves for work or education
   b. The place you live
   c. The spaces you occupy during daily activity, including your home and work
   d. Large regional cities offering services

20. The same land in England has been occupied by various populations. You might, in an archaeological dig, find the remnants of early Britons, Romans, Vikings and later peoples. This is an example of:
   a. Contagious diffusion
   b. Relocation diffusion
   c. Sequent occupancy
   d. Cultural ecology

21. A culture complex consists of:
   a. A number of cultural systems
   b. A number of cultural traits
   c. Multiple culture regions
   d. Multiple regional identities

22. Mecca is an example of a cultural hearth. The spread of Islam from Mecca outward is:
   a. Expansion diffusion
   b. Hierarchical diffusion
   c. Contagious diffusion
   d. Relocation diffusion

23. Identify the difference between a ghetto and an economic enclave.
   a. An ethnic enclave has a high concentration of a given ethnicity and may be a ghetto.
   b. Individuals of a single ethnicity are forced to live in ghettos by political or economic conditions. Ethnic enclaves are entirely voluntarily inhabited communities.
   c. Both ghettos and ethnic enclaves have residents of a single ethnicity; however, living in a ghetto is not voluntary. Ethnic enclaves may be ghettos or simply ethnic neighborhoods.
   d. Ghettos are poor neighborhoods. Ethnic enclaves are wealthier.

24. Choose the best definition of maladaptive diffusion.
   a. Maladaptive diffusion occurs when traits from the original culture are replaced with traits from another culture.
   b. Maladaptive diffusion occurs when popular culture replaces folk culture.
   c. Maladaptive diffusion occurs when cultural traits are adopted, even if they do not function well.
   d. Maladaptive diffusion occurs when two equal cultures swap or share traits.

25. The caste system is part of:
   a. Buddhism
   b. Hinduism
   c. Judaism
   d. Sikhism

26. Mecca is to Muslims as _____ is to Hindus.
   a. The Indus
   b. The Ganges
   c. Bangladesh
   d. India

27. Shintoism is common in:
   a. Japan
   b. India
   c. Nepal
   d. Thailand

28. Which of the following is contributing to conflicts between India and Pakistan?
   a. Allocation of resources
   b. Religion
   c. Border delimitation
   d. Ethnic differences

29. **In which of the following states is a conflict between Islam and Christianity currently impacting the population?**
    a. Israel
    b. Palestine
    c. Nigeria
    d. India

30. **There is a stateless nation in Iraq. That nation is:**
    a. Palestine
    b. Sunni
    c. Shi'ite
    d. Kurdistan

31. **The proto-tongue or mother-tongue is:**
    a. Written language
    b. The first spoken language
    c. The language of Mesopotamia
    d. The first Indo-European language

32. **How many individual language families are there?**
    a. More than 200
    b. More than 100
    c. More than 50
    d. More than 15

33. **The language family with the greatest number of speakers is:**
    a. Sino-Tibetan
    b. Indo-European
    c. Afro-Asiatic
    d. Niger-Congo

34. **The most common Indo-European language is:**
    a. Spanish
    b. French
    c. Italian
    d. English

35. What is a toponym?

a. Two words that sound the same

b. Two words that sound different

c. A place name with religious meaning

d. A place name

36. Choose the example below that is an example of irredentism?

a. America's expansion westward in the 19th century

b. Hitler's invasion of Poland in 1939

c. America's involvement in Iraq following 9/11

d. The Taliban's activity in Afghanistan

37. Which of the following has been, in the past, a buffer zone?

a. Eastern Europe

b. Israel

c. Germany

d. The United Kingdom

38. Eastern Europe was, during the Cold War, referred to as:

a. The Rust Belt

b. The Sun Belt

c. The Shatter Belt

d. A buffer state

39. Prior to 1990, West Berlin was an example of:

a. An exclave

b. A proruption

c. An enclave

d. Both an exclave and an enclave

40. Which two European states were the largest colonial powers?

a. England and Germany

b. England and Belgium

c. England and France

d. England and Portugal

41. Which describes the domino theory?

    a. Countries that were former colonial properties will have difficulty succeeding without assistance.

    b. When a power gains land, it will continue to gain more land.

    c. Once one country becomes politically unstable, neighboring countries will.

    d. When colonialism ended, countries gained economic freedom and eventual development.

42. What is the possible impact of multiple core regions or cores within a single state?

    a. Improved unity

    b. Disunity

    c. Better infrastructure

    d. Improved social conditions

43. Why would a more-developed country have a primate city, commonly found in less developed countries?

    a. Because the city is a center of economic power

    b. Because the city has a very long history

    c. Because of cultural power

    d. Because of political power

44. Which of the following is an example of a forward capital?

    a. St. Petersburg

    b. Rio de Janeiro

    c. New York City

    d. Paris

45. The Pledge of Allegiance is an example of a :

    a. Centrifugal force

    b. Pull factor

    c. Push factor

    d. Centripetal force

46. **The first form of planting was likely:**
    a. Seeds
    b. Vegetative plantings from cuttings
    c. Transplanting natural seedlings
    d. Accidental, as plants grew from waste

47. **The most important phase of the Second Agricultural Revolution occurred during:**
    a. The Roman Empire
    b. The Middle Ages
    c. The Industrial Revolution
    d. World War II

48. **Victory gardens or kitchen gardens were of particular importance during what period due to food shortages and rationing?**
    a. World War I
    b. World War II
    c. The Industrial Revolution
    d. The early 20th century

49. **When land lies fallow it is:**
    a. Planted
    b. Not planted
    c. Planted with a different crop
    d. Used for animal pasture

50. **Which of the following is NOT true of subsistence farmers?**
    a. They sell excess goods at market
    b. They use slash-and-burn techniques
    c. They may use intertillage
    d. They can use crop rotation

51. **What is the most common crop in South China?**
    a. Millet
    b. Rice
    c. Wheat
    d. Soy

52. What has significantly reduced famine in the modern world?

    a. Millet

    b. Potatoes

    c. High-yield crops

    d. Organic food production

53. Which of the following might participate in a debt-for-nature swap?

    a. The International Monetary Fund

    b. The World Health Organization

    c. The United Nations

    d. OPEC

54. Political leaders belong to what sector of employment:

    a. Primary

    b. Secondary

    c. Tertiary

    d. Quinary

55. Which of the following has experienced significant industrialization most recently?

    a. France

    b. The United Kingdom

    c. China

    d. Japan

56. Where did early industries develop?

    a. In major cities

    b. Near coal deposits

    c. In open countryside

    d. Near train depots

57. Who proposed the theory of Least Cost?

    a. Von Thunen

    b. Wallerstein

    c. Mackinder

    d. Weber

58. Which of the following is an example of agglomeration?
    a. A shoe company builds a new factory in a Special Economic Zone in China
    b. A clothing company opens a plant in the United States, in the founder's hometown
    c. A food company locates near its major growing regions
    d. Multiple manufacturers share a large space in an industrial park, with easy access for trucks, loading, unloading and utilities

59. Chose the theory that would support the following statement: Colonial powers used natural resources, but left little infrastructure in less-developed countries.
    a. World Systems Theory
    b. Least Cost Theory
    c. Dependency Theory
    d. Domino Theory

60. Special Economic Zones are designed to make the region appealing to:
    a. Workers
    b. Local businesses
    c. Multinational corporations
    d. Tourists

61. Which of the following is NOT part of the Pacific Rim economic region?
    a. China
    b. Singapore
    c. Japan
    d. North Korea

62. What was the primary function of a colonial city?
    a. Political stability
    b. Religious center
    c. Cultural center
    d. Export center

63. **What is the largest forced migration in history?**
    a. The African slave trade
    b. The Trail of Tears
    c. The expulsion of the Jews from Spain
    d. The movement of prisoners of war to Siberia

64. **Medieval Europe organized various types of professionals into labor guilds. The districts associated with these guilds created:**
    a. Urban planning
    b. Zoning
    c. Walled cities
    d. Grid layouts

65. **Urbanization increased significantly:**
    a. During the 1400s
    b. During the 1600s
    c. During the 1800s
    d. During the 900s

66. **In which of the following cities might you expect to find squatter settlements?**
    a. Chicago, Illinois
    b. Quebec, Montreal
    c. London, England
    d. Rio de Janeiro, Brazil

67. **Both Von Thunen and Christaller assume what about cities?**
    a. Cities are spread over a large area
    b. Cities will have distinct geographical features
    c. Cities will be placed on rivers
    d. Cities will be flat, without barriers

68. **The rural people living around a city are referred to, according to Christaller, as:**
    a. Suburbanites
    b. The hinterland
    c. Commuters
    d. Labor force

69. **Which of the following is the best definition of threshold, with regard to urban planning?**
    a. The number of people required to form a city
    b. The number of people required to form an edge city
    c. The number of people required to support a business or service
    d. The number of people required to form a community

70. **Which theory of development predicts hexagonal development?**
    a. Van Thunen
    b. Domino theory
    c. Christaller
    d. Wallerstein

71. **Which of the following would be near the top of an urban hierarchy?**
    a. Miami, Florida
    b. Los Angeles, California
    c. Columbia, Missouri
    d. Indianapolis, Indiana

72. **What is the most essential function of a world city?**
    a. Finance
    b. Communication
    c. Culture
    d. Industry

73. **A city with a population over 10 million is:**
    a. Urban
    b. Primate city
    c. World city
    d. Megacity

74. **According to Borchert, a stage 4 city:**
    a. Developed before 1810
    b. Developed during the middle of the 19th century
    c. Developed during the late 19th century
    d. Developed during the early 20th century

75. Edge cities are likely to develop:

    a. From earlier villages

    b. Along highway exits

    c. Far away from major cities

    d. In the center of the city

Free-Response Questions

1. Explain Von Thunen's Model. Include his reasoning, his views on land use, and discuss the flaws of his model.

2. Discuss the development of agriculture and the changes brought about in terms of culture and land use following the First Agricultural Revolution.

3. Discuss the five major sectors of employment, explaining what occupations fall into each and how these might relate to an understanding of classification of countries as "more or less developed."

Answer Key 1

Multiple-Choice

1. B	26. D	51. B
2. A	27. D	52. C
3. A	28. A	53. A
4. A	29. B	54. C
5. B	30. A	55. D
6. A	31. D	56. C
7. D	32. A	57. B
8. D	33. C	58. B
9. C	34. A	59. A
10. D	35. B	60. A
11. C	36. C	61. D
12. B	37. A	62. D
13. A	38. B	63. A
14. D	39. C	64. B
15. A	40. B	65. D
16. C	41. C	66. B
17. D	42. D	67. A
18. D	43. A	68. B
19. C	44. D	69. B
20. B	45. C	70. D
21. A	46. C	71. C
22. B	47. D	72. B
23. B	48. C	73. B
24. A	49. C	74. D
25. A	50. B	75. D

Free-Response

1. The population pyramid for the Ukraine provides a number of details about their demographics, and even allows for a number of possible scenarios with regard to economic development, culture, and political organization. The population pyramid provides information about birth rates, general fertility rate, dependency ratio, life expectancy and any population disparities regarding gender.

    Birth rates in the Ukraine have been progressively and slowly increasing after a distinct drop 10-14 years ago. While they are increasing, the overall birth rate is quite low, judging by this population pyramid, particularly in comparison to the past. The fertile population, or women between 15 and 45 is quite high, suggesting high overall fertility at this time. This factor alone cannot explain the increasing birth rate, so it may be the result of other social or cultural factors. Economic factors and political instability may be contributing to an overall decline in population.

    The dependency ratio is rather low, with a majority of the population falling between 15 and 64 years of age. This is the result of both a low birth rate and a low life expectancy, particularly for men. The population is relatively evenly distributed through age 55, but then a clear gender disparity appears. This suggests that female lifespans are significantly longer than male lifespans in the Ukraine. Were this drop to occur in early adulthood, we might theorize war or a similar issue, but in this case, it suggests health-related issues. These appear in the Ukraine at a quite high rate, given the gender disparity and the age which it appears. Lifestyle issues, like smoking, are likely to play a role in this.

    Overall, this population pyramid suggests, just from the numbers, that conditions are not positive in the Ukraine. The population appears to be shrinking, rather than maintaining itself, and people are not choosing to have children at a replacement rate. Life expectancy is low, suggesting poor social conditions overall. The statistical information in this pyramid supports current events in the Ukraine, which suggest both political unrest and economic struggles. While in a less-developed country, a high birth rate typically correlates with poor social conditions, access to contraceptives in the former Soviet Union is good, so women are able to control their fertility in response to the world around them.

2. While immigration rates through the late 18th century were relatively low, from the middle of the 19th century through the early 20th century, immigration rates increased dramatically, with most immigrants coming to the United States from Europe. While individuals certainly had their own reasons for immigrating, a number of broad factors made the decision more likely during this period. Push factors are those things in the home country that encourage emigration, while pull factors are desirable traits about the new location.

In Europe, unemployment was high, a number of countries experienced significant famine, and, in some areas, there were still few opportunities outside of farming and agricultural life. The specific push factors varied from region to region. For instance, the Irish potato famine of the 1840s encouraged significant emigration, as people sought out a more stable financial situation and reliable food. In Italy, following unification in 1892, political instability led many Italians to seek a better life in the United States. In much of Eastern Europe, political instability also contributed to a desire for a better life. Hungarians immigrated in large numbers both early in the 20th century and again following World War I. People left poor job outlooks, inadequate food, intolerance and political instability for new opportunity.

The United States had a number of desirable traits available for immigrants. For farmers who wished to work the land, homesteading laws in the newly opened West in the 19th century made land ownership feasible. For others, the appeal of jobs in America's industrialized cities was a pull factor for immigration. Relatively early, many groups established cultural enclaves, providing familiar churches, language and foods for immigrants, particularly in cities like New York. Additionally, for some, immigration to the United States provided religious freedom, drawing, for instance, many Russian Jews to New York prior to the Bolshevik Revolution. Immigrant communities provided stability and support, while industry and land meant the possibility of financial success. The Constitution provided protections against pogroms and other forms of discrimination. Fundamentally, these pull factors can be summed up as the potential for a better life.

The U.S. provided land, opportunity, income, and freedom for many, welcomed to Ellis Island throughout this period of significant immigration. For those without strong family support, their first years were often difficult ones; however, close-knit communities helped to provide for new immigrants, assisted with jobs and housing and more.

3. The Demographic Transition Theory provides a model for changing populations as societies modernize, industrialize and urbanize. While this theory provides some general guidelines regarding population growth and eventual stabilization, it has several significant flaws that make it less useful than it might seem at first.

The Demographic Transition Theory is based on the demographics of Western Europe, from the pre-industrial era through relatively modern times. Stage one is pre-industrial, and stage four may be read as today. While this model may be true for Western Europe, one must question whether the experiences of a single society with regard to population demographics are applicable to all societies.

In some societies, including Southern Europe, the birth rate declined well before mortality rates did. The Demographic Transition model posits a decline in birth rate in stage 3, with a decline in mortality beginning in stage 2. Furthermore, declining birth rates varied from country to country due to multiple factors, including urbanization.

This theory fails to account for unusual changes in population, including those due to war. For instance, the post-World War II baby boom does not, in any way, fit into stage 4 as described by this theory. Other factors, outside of development, may impact birth and mortality rates in significant ways. This also does not account for epidemic illnesses, like AIDS and their impact.

The Demographic Transition Theory assumes that all societies will proceed through all four stages of development, without interruption. Today, much of the less-developed world remains in one of the early stages, with little evidence of transition. Mortality has declined and the birth rate remains high. This has led to an increasing population, making economic development much more difficult, if not impossible. According to the Demographic Transition Theory, economic development will reduce the birth rate; however, with a growing population, that development cannot occur.

While this theory may provide a useful model for how population patterns changed in relatively limited conditions, we do need to understand its limits and where it should, and should not, be applied. The model may be historically useful, but as modern experiences in the less developed world show, it has not been proven by experience.

Answer Key 2

Multiple-Choice

1. C	26. A	51. C
2. C	27. D	52. B
3. A	28. C	53. A
4. A	29. C	54. C
5. C	30. A	55. A
6. B	31. A	56. B
7. A	32. C	57. C
8. B	33. B	58. A
9. A	34. D	59. C
10. A	35. D	60. D
11. C	36. D	61. A
12. D	37. D	62. D
13. A	38. A	63. C
14. C	39. B	64. B
15. D	40. C	65. A
16. B	41. B	66. B
17. C	42. D	67. B
18. C	43. A	68. A
19. C	44. D	69. C
20. C	45. D	70. C
21. D	46. D	71. B
22. D	47. B	72. C
23. D	48. B	73. B
24. A	49. C	74. D
25. A	50. C	75. B

Free-Response

1. Religion has fueled political conflicts for centuries as groups argue over the use of land, rights to holy sites and other factors. Today, religion is at the center of a number of significant political conflicts, including those in Nigeria, India, Iraq, and Israel. The conflict in Nigeria is escalating, with some fears that it may lead to genocide amidst current widespread violence.

    The tribes of Nigeria are not only divided by culture and history, but also by religion. In the south, Christianity, brought by European missionaries, is dominant. In the northern part of the country, the majority of the tribes are Islamic. A relatively small percentage of the population continues to practice native African religions. Religious tensions between Muslims and Christians have contributed to the conflicts in Nigeria. While the leader of Boko Haram claims to be Muslim, Muslim leaders in Nigeria have publicly denounced his violent activities.

    Under the British colonial government, the south, and Christian tribes, were favored over the north. Christian missionaries built schools and created an educational system that is contrary to the values of radical Islamic militants. Furthermore, tribes in the south were allowed more self-governance than those in the north, contributing to resentment. The terrorist organization, Boko Haram, has already begun to target schools, particularly those teaching girls, for acts of violence.

    The modern Nigerian state is formally a democracy, but allegations of corruption are common. The country has had difficulty developing a functional government because of the diversity of ethnic and religious issues in the country. The lack of a stable government has created an environment that allows for terrorist groups and activity, like that of Boko Haram. Radical leaders affiliated with Boko Haram have claimed that the government has not only discriminated against members of the Hausa-Fulani tribe, but has engaged in ethnic cleansing and substantial violence against Muslims in the region.

    The culmination of these tensions is a nation in near-crisis. International authorities, including developed nations, have offered assistance in combating violence in Nigeria; however, solutions remain unclear. Religion, including the conflict between westernized Christians and fundamentalist Islam, is at the heart of this conflict, alongside longstanding ethnic tensions.

2. Geopolitical theories attempt to explain the political use of space. These theories have varied widely over time, in response to politics and changing technology; however, they have all dramatically impacted political action while in favor.

The German Ratzel identified states as organic bodies who sought growth or "raum". As a social Darwinist, Ratzel applied his own interpretation of Darwinism to politics. The strongest states would survive, conquering and taking land from weaker states to improve themselves. Under Adolf Hitler, the German state embraced the idea of "lebensraum" or living space, using it to justify actions against Czechoslovakia and Poland.

Mackinder believed that that Heartland or Eurasia was the most critical power in the world. The state controlling this part of the world would control the entire world. Sea power was critical to maintain this support and maintain this control. The British, and prior to World War I, the Germans embraced this idea, working to build a large navy. During World War I, the desire for control of the Heartland was key to German wartime goals. With the introduction of air power, this theory became less relevant. The Heartland was no longer the safest region. Also, as the U.S. grew into a superpower, Mackinder's theory became rather misplaced and unimportant.

Following World War II, Europe was divided into East and West. Eastern Europe was controlled by the communist Soviet Union and communism was making gains elsewhere in the world, including in Southeast Asia. The domino theory stressed the importance of preventing those gains, even at a high cost. NATO was created to prevent the spread of communism into Western Europe, and wars in Korea and Vietnam were the result of the domino theory.

Political theory can have a substantial impact on political action, whether that theory provides a structure for actions already desired, a justification for actions, or even a reason for worry. These theories have shaped the world during the course of the 20th century.

3. The city of Paris is today a modern capital of fashion and a significant historical site. Like many early cities, Paris is situated on a river, with an accessible, central location. While it is a fashion power and a cultural center, Paris is not a primate city or a world city today.

Inhabited for centuries, the city of Paris began as a fishing village on the river Seine. It grew in size during the Roman occupation of France, but remained relatively unimportant until the Middle Ages. Paris became the capital of a growing state in the early Middle Ages, under the rule of the Capetians. By the high Middle Ages, the city was a prominent home to a well-known university, Cathedral and had become a center of culture. French was even the language of the cultured in Western Europe for some time. The city was later the center of the French Revolution and then home to Napoleon. The lively spirit and personality of Paris perseveres to this day in its culture, history and character.

Like other medieval cities, Paris was characterized by crowded buildings, narrow streets and alleys, and a general lack of hygiene. Space to bury the dead was limited, leading to the use of underground catacombs. Eventually, the general dirt and crowding in the city led to the creation of a large palace complex some miles from the city, in Versailles. This does not, in any way, resemble the city so loved today.

Under Napoleon III in the middle of the 19th century, the city underwent a clear urban revitalization project or, in more modern terms, gentrification. Overcrowded neighborhoods were torn down, new buildings and wider streets constructed, along with large public parks. While this made the city much prettier, it also created poor settlements along the outskirts of the city. These changes created the city center we recognize today. A visitor can stroll along these streets and see the impact of urban planning and zoning on the city. Even today, the city planning that went into place in the 19th century improves traffic in the city center in Paris, designed long before the first cars drove on these boulevards.

While Paris is not a political power today, it is a cultural one. Home to iconic monuments, from the Cathedral of Notre Dame to the Eiffel Tower, the city is vibrant, carrying its own distinctly French personality.

Answer Key 3

Multiple-Choice

1. C	26. B	51. B
2. D	27. A	52. C
3. C	28. B	53. A
4. C	29. C	54. D
5. C	30. D	55. C
6. B	31. B	56. B
7. B	32. D	57. D
8. B	33. B	58. D
9. B	34. A	59. C
10. D	35. D	60. C
11. B	36. B	61. D
12. A	37. A	62. D
13. C	38. C	63. A
14. B	39. D	64. B
15. B	40. C	65. C
16. A	41. B	66. D
17. C	42. B	67. D
18. B	43. B	68. B
19. C	44. A	69. C
20. C	45. D	70. C
21. B	46. B	71. B
22. A	47. C	72. B
23. C	48. B	73. D
24. C	49. B	74. D
25. B	50. A	75. B

Free-Response

1. Von Thunen created a model to explain land use around the city in pre-industrial times. This model was designed to consider various functional issues, including space, transportation and food storage, as well as the most efficient use of space.

   Von Thunen's model focuses on transportation as the primary issue when considering land use. Food and other goods must be transported into the city, by oxcart, as his theory predates rail. This model is visualized as something like a target, in which the city itself is the bull's eye. Directly surrounding the city are food production facilities for highly perishable goods, including dairies and vegetable gardens.

   Just outside this first ring around the city, the next ring around the city would produce lumber. Lumber was costly to transport, so production near the city center reduced cost for the buyer and seller. Farms to grow grain for human and animal use made up the next ring. Grain used for animals did not need to be near the city center, and grain was slow to spoil, so could be growth further away. Finally, the final ring allowed for livestock and ranching activities. Livestock could be walked into town and butchered in town, limiting high transportation costs. The final section was, by Von Thunen, considered to be wilderness, too far from the city to serve a valuable function.

   Von Thunen's model is only relevant in specific situations. First and foremost, it assumes a pre-industrial environment. While most cities have access to a waterway, Von Thunen does not consider it a potential means of transit for goods, like lumber. Furthermore, the city is assumed to lie on a plain, with no geographical features that might impact the use of land. In many cases, soil quality, climate and other factors play a bigger role in the use of land than transportation distances. Also, this presumes an isolated city, rather than one with other communities near by which might access the same services.

   This is a model of agricultural land use, but one that may not consistently apply or may not apply at all. Understanding this model of land use may help you to recognize patterns in pre-industrial Europe, but should not be held to be universally true.

2. The development of agriculture during the First Agricultural Revolution changed the way humans lived, eventually leading to the development of cities, urban life, written language, and new technologies.

Prior to the Agricultural Revolution, humans lived in relatively small groups, surviving by hunting and gathering local foods. The ability to prepare for future harvests by saving cuttings or seeds, to intentionally produce food and to store food, like grain, for future use enabled a new lifestyle. For the first time, humans could settle in villages to raise their food, rather than moving as they depleted a food supply.

With the introduction of villages, a new social hierarchy and control developed. People now lived in bigger groups and required more organization to delegate labor and distribute food. With new technology, fewer people were needed to produce food. This freed up individuals to develop metal and pottery technology, improve building techniques or serve a religious function. This trend began in as villages grew, eventually leading to the development of the city.

New technology, new crops and animal domestication led to an improved food supply and less risk of famine. Furthermore, settlements made it easier to care for children, helping to support an increased birth rate. Over time, this increased birth rate increased the general fertility rate and led to much larger human populations. Cities grew in size, but also spread the population as people moved to found new cities.

While the early cities were relatively few in number, information about agriculture, technology and religion spread through expansion diffusion. Eventually, the first cities led to the first political empires, like those of the Assyrians and Babylonians. The leaders of these cities founded new cities, and, in some cases, those cities went on to found new cities.

A single simple innovation, the choice to grow food intentionally, created massive and lasting social change in every aspect of human life. Houses replaced caves and temporary shelters of animal skins. Larger houses, civic buildings, and temples created social hierarchies. The need for food distribution, government and record-keeping led to systems of accounting and writing. Each of these innovations required the existence of a stable food supply and the freedom to pursue other word, created through the use of agriculture.

3. Types of employment may be divided into five different sectors. These sectors are relevant for both more and less developed societies; however, the proportion of individuals employed in a given sector will vary depending upon development.

The primary sector describes jobs in agriculture, food production and resource collection. In a less-developed country, the majority of the population will work in primary sector occupations. These include farming, mining, and lumber. For a country with oil reserves, oil drilling is also an example of a primary sector job. The number of people employed in primary sector jobs drops in a more-developed state.

The secondary sector is manufacturing or construction. This is the process of turning raw materials into a finished product. This includes both heavy and light industry and may be used domestically, by other industries or exported for sale. The introduction of manufacturing is a step in the industrialization process.

The tertiary sector consists of service-oriented jobs. This includes everything from banking to teaching to medicine to customer service of various sorts. In a more-developed society this makes up the majority of the available jobs, in one context or another. In some analyses, this is the final sector, with all more educated or "white-collar" jobs grouped into the tertiary sector.

More complex analyses add a quaternary and quinary sector. The quaternary sector includes information services of all sorts, while the quinary includes politicians and others in the ruling elite. Growth in both of these sectors is also expected alongside economic development.

It is critical to understand that even in a less-developed country, some number of jobs in other sectors exist. To use these qualifications to judge economic development, you must consider the proportion of jobs, not their very existence. For instance, in the U.S. today, a large number of people work in information technologies of one sort or another. In Nigeria, that would be a much smaller percentage of the working population. As countries develop, more of the labor force moves up to work in a higher sector of employment.

Image References

1. Map of the world from the *World Factbook.* Public domain.
2. Map of Africa from Wikimedia Commons. Public domain.
3. Map of Latin America from Wikimedia Commons. Public domain.
4. Map of Europe from Wikimedia Commons. Public domain.
5. Map of Asia from Wikimedia Commons. Public domain.
6. Map of North America from Wikimedia Commons. Public domain.
7. Population Pyramid from Wikimedia Commons. Public domain.
8. Population Change and Demographic Transition from Wikimedia Commons. Public domain.
9. Passage of ships from Africa to North and South America from Wikimedia Commons. Public domain.
10. Language families around the world from Wikimedia Commons. Public domain.
11. Religion distribution around the world from Wikimedia Commons. Public domain.
12. Image of "geographic pivot" from *The Geographical Pivot of History* by Halford Mackinder. Public domain.
13. Spread of agriculture from Wikimedia Commons. Public domain.
14. Von Thunen's model from Wikimedia Commons. Public domain.
15. Arable land around the world from Wikimedia Commons. Public domain.
16. GDP by country from Wikimedia Commons. Public domain.
17. Economic growth by country from Wikimedia Commons. Public domain.
18. Fertility rate by country from Wikimedia Commons. Public domain.
19. Greenhouse gas emissions by country from Wikimedia Commons. Public domain.
20. Human Development Index by country from Wikimedia Commons. Public domain.
21. Map of United States from Wikimedia Commons. Public domain.
22. Map of African slave trade from Wikimedia Commons. Public domain.
23. Ukrainian population pyramid from Wikimedia Commons. Public domain.
24. The demographic transition model from Wikimedia Commons. Public domain.

Made in the USA
Columbia, SC
30 June 2019